FROM
PARADISE
TO
EDEN

Dulcie Matthews

Pen Press Publishers Ltd

First published in Great Britain by
Pen Press Publishers Ltd
39-41, North Road
Islington
London N7 9DP

ISBN 1-904754-56-2

Printed and bound in the UK

Also by Dulcie Matthews
RIOT OF THORN AND LEAF
Hayloft

A catalogue record of this book is available from
the British Library

Cover design Jacqueline Abromeit
from original drawings by Brett Matthews-Tipper
photographs by Garry Tipper and Philip Baskerville

For my Grandchildren
Sally, Alex, Gemma and Daniel. My Great-grandchildren
Darcy, May and Thomas, and for those as yet unborn.
Also for my dearly loved Big Brother.

About the author

Dulcie was born in Paradise, Coventry just two years before the outbreak of the Second World War. She grew up during the Blitz, and watched as her city rose from the ashes to build and thrive again. She attended Stoke Park Grammar school, going on to do office work before working in Social Services. In 1987 she left Coventry to live in Cumbria.

She now lives in a small Cumbrian village with her husband and four cats.

These are her memories; others will have different recollections because life itself is faceted, changing in perception when viewed from a different place. The events that take place are real, but the names have been changed in some instances to protect anonymity.

In and out the winding alleys,
In the back streets and the dirt.
Small despairing scruffy children,
Running nose and ragged shirt.

Eyes look downward to the pavement,
Seeing only grime and dust.
Mud and brick-ends are their playthings,
Walls that fall, and gates that rust.

Houses, leaning on each other
Tiny yards where flowers won't grow.
Spilling dustbins, hopeless people,
All the world they'll ever know.

In and out the winding alleys,
Kicking tins, not asking why.
Small despairing scruffy children,
Please look up and see the sky.

Prologue

What is this strange thing that we are? We burst into life through pain, like shooting stars, created and dying through millennia of time into the Universe. For a brief moment, we shine as we dance, make music, climb mountains. Then we plunge into the depths of eternal obscurity, our brief span is over; there is nothing left of our pain, our joy, our achievement and failure. This odd miracle of humanity wherein we experience laughter, love and hate, brilliance and pain, just as suddenly ends – we are no more, our brilliance has gone. Why did it exist at all? Why can humankind reach such sublime heights and yet be capable of plummeting bottomless depths? Where does the awareness, the knowing, begin?

She sat in her mother's chair watching rainbows fall onto her hands. Stiff hands that would no longer obey her, but now lay in her lap, skin stained brown. Dry skin stretched across fragile bones. They twitched, out of her control, trembled like dry autumn leaves when she reached for her cup. The cup with a handle on each side – no flowers on it to make it special, not china the way she liked, just blue plastic. This is how it was now that she was old. Nothing special like china cups, what would be the point? She would only drop it, wouldn't she. Now she wasn't spoken to, only 'about' – just like being a child.

But thoughts? Now that was something else altogether. She had many thoughts, they deafened her. Her head was full of a constant endless stream of them. They held a dialogue with her memory, pulling out long forgotten times, people, places. There was no problem with the past, but the present was an unreality. 'Has she taken her pills today?' Why didn't they ask *her*? Not that she could remember. Better to keep quiet or they would get cross with her again, and then she would become flustered, apologetic. Her thoughts drifted away from the room. Who was the small girl? She felt sure it was her daughter. But – it couldn't be, could it? Who was it then...? So she sat, silent in the silent afternoon, watching the rainbows move slowly across her hands.

The old lady watched the child; She saw the familiar way the small girl turned rhythmically to the music, holding her skirts at each side. She was singing; what *was* that song? '*You are my sunshine...*' She knew it; she tried to join in, and a trickle of dribble slid without control from the corner of her mouth. The room, the child, all began to fade, to merge into something else, and the old lady slept, as rainbows moved across her face.

The Valley of Eden

Life is a cycle – a series of ends and beginnings. There cannot be the one without the other. I am beginning at the end – which isn't really the end, but just a pause in my journey. Do we ever reach the destinations we set out for, or is it instinct, accident? For eleven years I lived in a gentle back-stream of trees, sharing my daily life with deer, shrews, moles, slugs and cats. Each day I watched the sea reflect the seasons. I revelled in its changing moods, as sun rested on waves, storms rode in on the wind. Nights were alive with the calls of owls, the soft sound of oystercatchers on a flooded field. A becalmed ship, I floated through each day and each experience, happy to live, to savour the moment – until a sudden rush of instinct aided by circumstance flooded me into the mainstream once again.

Now here I am in this present stage of a journey. The valley of Eden, magnificent, strong and indomitable. These hills have withstood time itself. They were here millions of years ago; they will be here when my journey is over. Will I then be a star that falls in the night sky, resting on their summit? Farms built of grey stone grow out of the landscape, making me feel safe and yet ever aware of my impermanence.

This is Eden; a delicate November sun is resting on the hills that stand guard over Lake Haweswater. It rests within the curve of each valley, outlining shapes, then slides sinuously downwards, leaving dark shadows sitting in hollows. Kidsty pike rises above fields that are now flooding with gold.

I am unprepared for the immovable strength and splendour of my surroundings. I am also unprepared for the gentleness – days when soft light and soft sunshine enfold the village and surrounding hills, giving grey stone walls a mellow warmth and the fields a timeless stillness.

I am a stranger here, with my origins in the city of Coventry and the soft rolling countryside of Wiltshire, but this village has welcomed me in. Not even from the first moment have I been made to feel like an 'offcomer'. This is a tight well-knit community with bonds stretching backwards in time to when the Vikings were here, and farther backward still into the prehistoric age, and the turbulence of its beginnings. Huge stones remain in fields, and embedded into garden walls, a reminder that there was once a stone circle at each end of the village with an avenue of stones linking them together. Our house must lie within its lines, telling me that my own journey is no more than the faintest blinking of an eye in the passage of time.

Nearby in the boundary of the Lake District lies Lake Haweswater, a reservoir that was created when the village of Mardale was flooded in 1937. Golden eagles nest there now, living in solitary splendour. Their safety dependant upon their splendid isolation, they soar in glorious freedom.

This is 2001; the year of the battle with Foot and Mouth disease. July and August are filled with the sounds of gunshot, of lorries trundling their grim loads to burning and burial sites. I draw the blinds, not wanting to see because to know is more than I can bear. Farm cats across the road wander aimlessly in the fields, treading delicately through early morning grass, looking for the sheep. Farmers still walk across their fields at first light. This is what they have always done, today is no different. So walls are repaired, fences mended. Hay for winter fodder is still gathered in, though for no purpose. The village and surrounding area await a New Year, still with the hope that has survived here since prehistoric times.

We have watched with despair as field after field has been emptied of life. Sad bunches of flowers hang on field gates, a tribute to death. Farmers who have farmed these fells for generations have lost more than stock; they have lost a way of life. They now gather in the village in small groups and talk. They have temporarily lost their purpose. What is there to get up for now? The Doctors' surgery becomes a place of consolation where more therapy is achieved whilst waiting than in the actual appointment.

'Has thee got flu?'

'They'll shoot thee.'

Such is the dry humour that deals with grief. True to the spirit of Cumbria, they already talk of re-stocking – of next year – and my admiration and love for these people increases even more as I listen. This is truly a wonderful place in which to live.

A new spring is here, and I walk with my daughter across fields looking for the first celandines. Life proceeds gently and with a pattern, which is comfortable

The world struggles with war, pain and fear, yet here we all are, living out each day, putting into it all we can. It was always thus, just as it was when I was a child running into air-raid shelters, and kicking shrapnel along city streets. As we walk along in companionable silence, I remember the place where I grew up. I am mentally dragged backwards into a vortex of time – spun and whirled through the years to a small back yard, back streets, drab wet pavements, and to the beginning of my journey…

Chapter One

When does memory first begin? Reaching inwards, I brush away mental cobwebs to see a baby in a pram. The smell of tar stirs a memory, and there I am, being pushed along, a piece of tar-soaked rope hanging on the hood. A similar piece of rope is hanging from my cot, and all I have to do to travel through the cobwebs is to smell tar as I pass roadworks!

Likewise, the smell of paraffin pushes me through the dusty tunnels of time to a place of silence, sudden noise – and fear…

The year is 1940, and I am three years old. Many things are happening, the details of which I will not know until years later. There is a war, and the city of Coventry is experiencing a blitz. I live in a terraced house sandwiched between factories that are prime targets for German bombers. All I know for now is that the world has become a frightening place filled with noise and uncertainty. I am woken from the security of sleep to the sound of a siren, bundled into coats, then taken to shelters.

But this night is different; we are huddled in the glory hole – a small cupboard under the stairs that is home to brooms, dusters and the gas meter. It is very small, and we are cramped. My brother, who is almost 13 years old, is here too. He tells me years later that he knew something was really wrong because Mum was giving us biscuits! He also says that I slept through it, but I remember being cold, feeling afraid, and loud noise that fills my head. The smell of the gas meter mingles with the Monday smell of polish and dusters. The glory-hole door is wedged across the opening and will not move. Mum is calling 'Sam!', but my Dad doesn't come. She is pushing the door, but then seems to give up and we settle down to wait. Maybe this is when I slept.

Now there are voices; I can hear the familiar sound of my dad's voice mingling with other voices. They are talking to my mother, and hands are pulling at the door, reaching in to us. More confusion, more bundling, darkness and noise. The smell of people's fear, and an air raid shelter. But which time am I remembering now? Searching around in this long disused room of my memory, there are many air-raid shelters. They all smell of paraffin, and I lie on a bunk close to a corrugated roof that is dripping condensation, the accumulated drops of liquid fear, onto my face. People huddle together, united by a common bond. They all seem to be talking at once, their words indistinguishable to me. The sound grows muffled, slowly fading into a drone. It is farther away now – softer, merging into an indistinct murmur, and I drift into sleep still straining to hear.

Sirens sound the 'all-clear; people spill out into the daylight shielding their eyes that have become accustomed to darkness. They are dazed sleepwalkers, not knowing what to expect. There is uneasy silence as they move slowly, anxiously – as in a dream, toward homes that may not still be standing. Picking their way through piles of bricks that are still sending up clouds of dust, they look for familiar landmarks, searching amongst the rubble for security.

As I grow older, I hear my mother and father talking about the Blitz. Mum tells me of the day after, when she walks into town along the Stoney Stanton Road. She needs to get to the Town Hall for ration books, but she has to pick her way through piles of bricks and devastation. My dreams are haunted by her descriptions of arms and legs, the 'bits' of people jutting from broken buildings. Of fires still burning, and nothing recognisable to her. I am eight years old before the war comes to an end, but at three, all I have are impressions – emotions coloured by sounds and smells, which after sixty-one years can still make me feel breathless and afraid of darkness.

We talk, my brother and I, in a precious rare moment together, and he tells me about the bomb which landed on the pavement outside our house. It didn't detonate, but the force of its landing causes the glory hole door to fall and wedge us in. He tells me how he looked at the parachute silk, noticing on his return home from the shelter in the morning that it has gone. He speculates idly as to its whereabouts. Parachute silk is a prized commodity, used to make blouses and lovely knickers! The war to him is an excitement. He is a 13-year-old boy, viewing everything from a different place, and he is able to find answers for the dark and the noise. When we talk, it is I who paint in the back cloth of sound, smell and feeling, while he adds the line drawings which complete the picture.

He tells me about 'Sids' shop. This shop is a part of our collective childhood, selling sweets in tall glass jars that line the window. The blast has shattered all the shop windows, leaving sweets scattered across the pavement.

This thirteen-year old sits on the kerb eating the unexpected bounty and waiting for his mother and baby sister to come home. He doesn't know where they are as they were separated on the way to the shelters, and our 15-year-old sister is somewhere else in the city with her friends. His Dad is fire watching, so he eats sweets until the uncertainty is over. He tells me about seeing our Dad walking towards him, and I feel his relief.

Events are running rapidly through my mind now; the door to my memory room is open wide. Memories are rushing out, but in their hurry to be born they become confused – their order, tangled. We are returning to the house from a shelter – but how old am I now? I notice doors hanging at funny angles; I am standing in my grey dressing gown with its tangled twisty cords. The windows are shattered, shards of glass are lying across the brown lino. There is no shine on the tabletop, only heavy grey-brown dust settled on its surface and hanging in the air, so that breathing makes me choke. There is no shine on the lino either, and my feet leave prints as I tread.

Now I am in a car that has an open top. Cars are unheard of where I live, so why am I in it? I shall never know, but I am looking at the devastation of a city. Everywhere there are piles of bricks, great craters where houses should have been, and people, standing around, not knowing quite what to do. I am sitting at a table with lots of people around it, and we are eating. As we never visit, this is a strange memory. There is a small boy of about seven or eight like me, and he is asking me to pass the 'winegar'. I correct him, and find I am in trouble. Later it is explained to me that this little boy is a German-Jew who has lost his family and I must be kind to him. This is a jigsaw of memory pieces, none of which fit together, and yet, laid out, they give a vivid picture of a time that has gone.

The war leaves strange benefits for a child who is only aware of the moment. There are huge gaps like open sores where houses should be. The piles of brick are mountains, and we climb them. They slide beneath our feet and we fall, but climbing is an adventure.. There are things to be discovered beneath them too. Plates, cups, pans, dolls, books, lie under rubble waiting to be unearthed.

The house at the end of the row is empty, and leans into the 'bombie'. This is our name for the open sores – this is our playground. The old lady isn't here any more, but we are Coventry war kids, living for the moment, oblivious to the misery, that has created our new world, so, we never wonder where she is. There is no glass in the windows, so we climb in. A few cut hands and knees make us careful as we drop onto the floor of the kitchen and kick away the broken glass. There is a teacup, a plate, a red plastic salt pot on the kitchen table, and something covered in furry green stuff, which smells awful. We wander around for a while, until we are discovered. Then there is much shouting about how wicked we are and how unsafe the house is. From then on, the house is boarded up, until it begins slowly to fall down, not in any spectacular way, but crumbling a few bricks at a time. As though it has got tired of waiting for the old lady to come home again.

In Crabmill Lane a large bomb has fallen, taking with it all the houses and leaving a huge crater. It is now a very large, natural stage, so we perform our impromptu concerts here. We take it in turns, no reluctance to do our bit, until our fingers and toes hurt with cold – yet still we stay. The crater is turning into scrub now; ragwort and dock pushing up hopeful shoots through broken bricks. Smaller craters make good dens with a roof made from dry twigs and brushwood. We smuggle out dry biscuits, anything we can find, and have 'tea parties', our feet sitting in cold wet mud as we share secrets, giggle about the mysterious facts of life.

It is Spring, and the shoots become flowers forcing their way between bricks on bomb sites. Buddhlia flourishes in walls, tassels of pink flowers spilling from crevices, growing over and through tumbledown walls. The odd brick, tired of hanging on, falls into the entry. Along the sides of the entry, the hawthorn is full of small white antiseptic smelling blossoms. We eat the tiny new leaves calling them 'bacon and eggs', then pick the blossoms to take home. Some mothers refuse to allow the flowers inside saying that they are bad luck, but my mother receives them gladly,, arranging them in a vase and placing them on the old oak table.

Kicking shrapnel along the street is another great way to pass the time. We spend long hours seeing which one can kick it the furthest, the one to reach the opposite gutter is the winner. Shoes already shabby and almost toeless become shabbier as the sharp pieces of metal tear into them.

It is a large piece of Shrapnel that takes a big part of our front step away. Years later, my brother tells me the story of the missing chunk. Dear old Dad was standing on it, watching the planes and listening for the sirens. Mum was following the usual routine at mealtimes of calling 'Sam!', and Dad was following the usual routine of ignoring her. Finally he decided to give in, at the same time as the piece of shrapnel took the lump from our step, missing him by inches!

Our lives are governed by ration books, and treats are rare. This makes the box of Mars bars in the corner of the back bedroom very tempting, almost unbearably tempting. Mum is going shopping – she sets off in her tweed coat, hair neatly rolled around her head and bag in her hand. I am left out in the street to play. This is my moment! We are always short of things – first they aren't there, and then, when they are we can't have them. They have to be limited – eked out and made to last. I climb through the pantry window which is a tight squeeze, Some heaving and struggling, a scratched knee, and I drop into the stone sink and onto the floor. Not considering any consequences and driven only by the need to have a chocolate bar, I go up to the back bedroom, take out the mars bars and begin to eat. The pleasure is indescribable, but the moment is brief. I hear the key turn in the back door and my heart thumps. My mother is back and I am in trouble again. I am a thief, I am deceitful, I cannot be trusted, I am greedy, and I don't deserve *anything*. But, with the taste of chocolate still in my mouth and a sick feeling in my stomach, it is worth it!

Our lavatory is in the yard, and I hate going because it is cold in the winter and dark at night. The paper is just newspaper, cut into squares and threaded onto a string. This is one of my jobs, to cut it and thread it. It is rough to use and leaves black stains on my bottom – another reason for not going to the toilet until the last minute. When in there, I sing very loudly, just to make myself feel safe.

The darkness is my biggest fear; the darkness follows me up the stairs and into my bedroom. Vampires lurk, and weird ghouls with evil eyes and blood dripping from fangs hang over me. All I can do is run, then bury my head into the covers, hoping that they will go away.

These are my formative years, forged from terror and uncertainty, loud bangs, sirens and rubble. Sounds and smells merging together – paraffin and wailing sirens, brick-dust and rubber. Gas masks, the stuff of nightmares – ugly and claustrophobic, turning familiar faces into monsters. As I write, I become breathless; the glory-hole with its fallen door shutting us in; air-raid shelters, my face almost pressing onto the clammy dripping corrugated roof that seems to be pressing down onto my face, thick dust cloying my nostrils. This is a world where fear clogs reason, noise numbs the mind, and dust chokes in the throat.

Chapter Two

After the war, the disused shelters remain standing, to rot slowly away. There is one in Edgewick Park, and we loiter around it, lost for things to do. It is a sinister relic, abandoned and of no further use, yet infinitely fascinating to us kids. We walk slowly down steps into the dark interior. We know there is water at the bottom – it lies there, dark-black and still. We know, even though we cannot see it, and the danger is exciting. Slowly down the dark steps we go, until there are no more steps, and water touches our feet. The smell is rotten and damp and our fingers slide on slimy corrugated iron walls in the darkness. We are told that there are rats here, but haven't seen any – so we look, with that delicious anticipation of being scared which is so peculiar to childhood.

Soon there is another distraction, as we see someone else hanging around the shelter. We call him 'Dirty Dick', and with the cruelty of youth, we follow him and chant his nickname. We are afraid of what we do not understand, yet cannot leave him alone. Dick is older than we are, and we know he is different.

It is the last few years of the war, and my bargaining position has improved, due to the American soldiers who are everywhere in Coventry. They wear smooth uniforms with a hat on the side of their head, and they speak in a funny way, sort of 'curly' and soft. They are very friendly, but my mother is suspicious and warns me to keep away. My sister Myrtle is now about seventeen, and very lovely. She has dark hair and green eyes, and she laughs a lot. She is going out with Len who lives in Eden Street, but a GI keeps coming to visit us. His name is Alan Goldberg, and when I see him walking down the Street, I run up to him so that he can pick me up and swing me around. My dad can't do this, as he only has one arm, so it's a treat. And Alan gives me sweets! We never see sweets, only the ones doled out at school when the Australian parcels arrive, so this is my bargaining material. The sweets are fruity and hard, in a tube with holes right through the middle, and I push them into my pockets, finding a place in the 'covered entry' to savour them secretly. I don't eat them, but return them to my pocket and hide them under my pillow later. Not having things makes me secretive, hiding away my treats to be enjoyed when they cannot be taken away from me. The other kids know that I have sweets because they see the American soldier pick me up and swing me round. Now they want me to play with them – suddenly I am popular. If I have two tubes, then I share one, but one is always hidden away to be savoured later.

Then Alan doesn't come any more, but I don't know why. Myrtle has gone away again in her ATS uniform, and Alan has gone too. There are no more sweets, or swings, and life is empty. Myrt isn't there singing around the house, and my brother isn't there either, as he is in the REME. There is less shouting too, as Dad didn't like Myrt going off with Alan because of her boyfriend Len, so Mum used to help Myrt to slip out sometimes without Dad knowing. I watch as a small girl watches, seeing the events, hearing the shouting, not understanding the politics. It is as though I am in a different world from theirs – they treat me as an amusement, a diversion, but mostly I am invisible.

At five, I am considerably younger than the other children in the Street, so I am able to tag onto the end of their groups without much opposition. Today, they are going to the Swanswell, which is a park with a large pool of water in its centre. It is a long way to the Swanswell, so they walk along the main road with me bringing up the rear and struggling to keep up. It takes a long time, as they push each other, kick stones, shout and argue. I keep quiet and just follow, as if I am too noisy, I will be sent back home.

'Buzz off, we don't want little kids with us…'

I ignore them, so they in turn ignore me. I am safe. Experience has already taught me that if I pretend not to care, they will get used to my presence. The important thing is not to talk. This I find the hardest of all!

The Swanswell is reached at last, and the games of chasing around the edges of the pool and jumping on each other from benches begin. I wander off to look at the grass and the ducks, and become lost in my own world. I look around for them, but they have gone. Tired of their games and totally unaware of me, they have simply walked home again. I am afraid, and so I cry. The world looks suddenly very big and very alien, and I don't know how to get home again.

I sit and cry for a long time, until the man approaches me. He is in that uniform like Alan wears, and his voice is soft and curly. I try to run, but somehow my legs won't work very well, and he is asking me why I am crying. I explain the story between sobs, and he gives me a large hankie, which I wipe my face on and give a big blow the way I have been told, and I feel a bit better. Then he lifts me up gently, which is a new experience. My experiences of being picked up are only of my brother, who likes to throw me into the air. This terrifies me, but it seems to please Clive, who is convinced that my yells are really from enjoyment. Mum laughs when Clive throws me up, and calls it being teased. But this man isn't throwing me anywhere; he is just lifting me up gently, and talking to me without shouting. He wipes black smudges from my face, and asks me 'Where do you live?' This is an easy one, as I know my address and feel very pleased to get something right.

'Silverton Road, Bell Green – I live in Paradise...' I speak clearly and with conviction. He walks with me and holds my hand, and we wait at the bus stop. The bus comes; he lifts me onto the platform, gives the conductor some money and explains to him where I live. What an adventure this is! Buses are a very rare treat, as legs were made before wheels. This must be right, as my Mother tells me so often.

I arrive home without even being missed, even though I have been gone for a very long time. Still, it is washing day, and the gate stays locked on washing day until every article has been washed, rinsed and mangled. This takes most of Monday, so my absence is not even noticed.

Chapter Three

There is nothing better than the treats enjoyed after there has been deprivation. Nothing better than to go without, and then to know good things. How can we ever appreciate the good without having known lack? This is how it is when the parcels arrive at school from Australia. The war is in its last year, and we still have no treats. When the parcels arrive, we are lined up in class, standing quietly behind each other around the large fireguard which protects us from the fire. In turn, no pushing, shoving or talking, we reach the front of the queue and we are handed one sweet. It is wrapped in shiny paper, and it goes into the depths of my pocket where I keep touching it secretly, waiting for the moment I can be alone and enjoy it.

The secretive pleasure of a treat savoured alone is something that has stayed with me throughout my life. The special chocolates, hidden in a drawer to be eaten when life is bad, or when no-one is there. Or worse, when life is *really* painful, the hoard of chocolate hidden under the bed.

Bananas are a casualty of war, not to be found anywhere. Myrtle draws me pictures of them, and I laugh. Mum describes them to me, but I cannot imagine such a funny thing. They look bent like an old person and not edible at all. There is whispering outside my bedroom door, and the door opens slowly. This is strange, as my Mum and my sister are laughing together excitedly. They make me sit up and close my eyes, then I hold out my hands, not one hand, but two. I run my fingers over the smooth shape before I open my eyes. They show me how to open it by peeling down the skin in four pieces. I put it very carefully into my mouth, because this could be what they call teasing again, and it could be nasty. My teeth sink into the soft pale flesh, and I savour the pleasure of the moment as I taste, for the first time, this thing called a banana.

Food is short, and our ration book rules our life. My mother makes us scrambled eggs with the pale yellow powder she has in the pantry. We use dried milk powder, and I watch her put vinegar into the cake mixture. There is 'spam' in tins, which is pink and tastes nice, and the cheese when we have it is rubbery. My mother calls it American cheese and says it is processed. I love the cheese, and like peeling away the shiny paper it is wrapped in. We are lucky, I am told, because Dad has his allotment, so we have fresh vegetables to eat.

My mother uses her old treadle sewing machine a lot. She used to make blackout curtains to shut out the light. This was to stop the enemy aeroplanes from seeing us, because if they saw lights they would drop bombs. We live in between factories so we are more at risk. She now makes our clothes from old bits of material. We need coupons to buy clothes with, so my mother 'makes do and mends' and nothing is wasted. I have blouses made from parachute silk and knickers made from Courtaulds fleece. This is like dusters and it itches my bottom.

The year is 1945, and the war is finally over. My friends' fathers are coming home again. They have been away for so long that I cannot remember them at all. My father has been a Home Guard because he was too old to go away. He was fighting in the First World War and he only has one arm so they don't want him.

Sylvia Faulkener's dad is coming home and we are all excited. He has been in Burma, and I think that it must be a very long way because it has taken him so long to get home again. I watch him walk up the Street; he is very brown, and walks slowly, bent like an old man. He has been in a Prisoner of War camp and is very ill. My parents talk in low voices about Mr Faulkener so that I can't hear them

In Bryn road there is a little girl called Veda Mickleskita, and I sometimes play with her in her garden. Her parents are very protective with her. My mother explains that Veda and her family have come to England to escape from tyranny. What a lovely word – 'tyranny'. I roll it about in my head and repeat it, not knowing what it means. I follow my mother into the kitchen.

'What is tyranny?'

'Oppression...'

'What is oppression?'

Constant questions usually get me into trouble, but this time I get an answer.

'Oppression is when people aren't free to be themselves. They are taken away to prison camps, starved, beaten and killed.'

I wander off to call for Veda, and to give this new horror some thought. Veda sings a little song that goes: 'Today I feel so happy, so happy, so happy. I don't know why I'm happy, I only know I am'. She must be happy because she is here in Coventry and not in oppression I think, but I still can't see *why* she is happy.

The war gave me new things to ponder on, different

playgrounds in which to stretch my imagination, and many unknown fears to deal with. It has left my world fractured, a tangled mess of deprivation, dust, noise and fear. But I survive, and move on into a world that becomes unaware of suffering. I watch the experience repeat itself so many more times in my journey through to Eden. As an adult I conclude that we never learn, and one generation can never pass on its experiences to another. Experience is something we all have to live through on our own.

Chapter Four

We spend so much time living in the past, or in an imagined future, that the present becomes the past almost without notice. As a child, I lived in the present, so when does it change, so that the present becomes just a waiting room for the future, a storehouse for memory. My life as a child should be simple, uncomplicated, yet it is a complex web of feeling, a helter-skelter of emotion and sensation, and its platform is the Street…

There isn't much to it really; just a row of red brick houses clinging to each other, leaning in against each other in a desperate bid for survival. Their doors open onto the street, their tiny gardens spill onto a communal entry. Gates hang on rusty hinges; dustbins spew their messy contents onto the pavements. My house has an entry running along its side, and a tiny front garden. It is the only one in the street with that honour, but to call it a front garden is an exaggeration.

The Street is a whole world; it is a stage on which many dramas are performed. It is still quiet today as I kick stones aimlessly into the gutter. The day has begun quite normally, with the usual tussle over hair brushing, the hurried dish of porridge and my mother's usual 'Go and play, I'm very busy'. The one very precious doll is placed carefully into the tiny wooden cart that serves as a pram. It is very important to be careful with the doll. Christina

Rossetti has a floppy rag body topped with a heavy chipped pot head. She has been given to me by Sylvia Faulkener's granny. Christina is the trusted confidante of many secrets, my friend and my comfort. This morning she is arranged in her 'pram' and I push her into the Street as I talk to her. I am feeling cross and something else – an emotion that I have no words for as yet. This morning I feel particularly in the way. My long hair is tangled, and the brush hurts. There is cleaning to do, dinner to cook, and a small girl who won't stand still and who will keep talking is an irritation to be dispensed with quickly.

So I skulk on the hard pavement, kicking stones, bending over Christina to pass on my secrets, then sit on the step. There is a big chunk of stone missing from the step where a bomb has hit it. It looks like a giant bite. No one else is out yet, so the distraction of the milkman's cart is very welcome. It trundles into the Street pulled by the huge brown horse. Bottles rattle as the cart jerks to a stop, and 'milkie' jumps down, securing the reins and reaching for the crate. 'Keep an eye out for Henry while I take these bottles, there's a good girl'. He disappears into the entry carrying an armful of bottles that make a clinking sound in the crate. I walk over to Henry, talking quietly to him. He smells nice, his brown flank is steaming with sweat. His big head bends towards me as I slowly and with purpose push my pram and Christina Rossetti under his legs. It feels safe under here, and the smell is even nicer, so I stand quite still and watch as the drama unfolds on the pavement. The milkman stares under Henry, and tells him to: 'stand'.

'Come on me duck, you'll do no good under there.' I listen to him intently, but I do not want to come out. It is nice under here, and now my mother has joined the milkman. They try everything; they coax, plead, and it all seems very funny. Quite a crowd has gathered there to see me defiantly standing under the horse. They bend down, peer under Henry, and the mood changes. My mother is now getting very angry and my feeling of safety dissolves.

The milkman saves the day. 'If you come out now, you can come on the cart to the end of the street, and give Henry his nosebag.' This sounds like a good deal, and it will also delay the moment of retribution when my mother must be faced. I walk slowly and carefully between Henry's legs and I am lifted onto the cart. Everyone disperses, the crisis is over. Mrs Roberts shuffles up the street, her slippers, trodden down at the back, flap as she walks. 'That one's a handful.' – 'She needs a slapped arse' – 'If you ask me, she wanders about too much for a little un.' These remarks are addressed to Mrs Stinchcombe who lives by the covered entry, before the women melt into their respective front doors, back to their scrubbing and their washing.

I walk back up the Street, my trip on the cart over. I now dawdle to delay the confrontation. It isn't yet dinnertime, and I know better than to go into the gate too soon, so I sit on the broken step to wait. Life is full of the unexpected, so when dinnertime arrives and my Dad comes to call me in, I don't greet the absence of anger with either surprise or relief. I seem to have escaped trouble this time and yet I would have welcomed it – at least it would have been a reaction. Life is funny, as I tell Christina Rosetti later.

Once a week the familiar shout of the Rag and Bone man causes scurrying in the Glory-hole for bags of discarded clothes and other bits and pieces. 'Rag 'n' Bones!' he shouts as he comes up the entry. He rattles the gates, and out they all come. Mrs Doulton, sharp-faced, brown and brisk, has her exchange of words with the huge dirty-looking man leaning over the gate. She laughs, tossing back her head, and I wonder what they are saying to each other. Mrs Evans comes out too. She is Kathy's mother. Kathy is my first real friend; she has always been here, even sharing a pram before we could walk. As my dusty layers of memory lift, she is there between each one, a continuing thread from past into future. She is happy and quick, never finding any idea too silly. She is very good at play-acting, making every game come to life. Sometimes she 'dies', throwing herself on the ground and staying there for ages, until I become worried and shake her. My mother tries to stop me from playing but doesn't tell me why. Grown up people are so silly. Kathys' mum always has time for me, she always listens, always has a cake or biscuit for me. In a future yet to come, it is Kathys' mum who helps me to bring my first born child into the world – but that is much later.

Next, it is Polly and Claras' gate. Polly and Clara Allsop are sisters, both very old, and very fat. They waddle up to the gate and hand over a bag of stuff. No laughs or chat – just a hand held out for the pence the Rag man pays. Clara has a red face and lots of chins, so that her face seems to join her body without room for her collar. Now it is our gate, and I am ready with the bag of clothes. I get to keep the pennies, so this means a trip to Sid's shop, which is a treat. The bag handed over, I run with the others, following the Raggie's progress up the Street. Sometimes, we run ahead of him, yelling 'Rag 'n' Bones!' up the entries, so that people can get their rubbish ready. Bedsteads, old chairs, clothes, all sorts of things are brought out to go on the cart, so that it wobbles and things fall from the back.

We run behind, retrieving and throwing them back on. Shirts, hats, and such an assortment of bric-a-brac lies in big piles, all to be sorted through.

The Rag and Bone man's cart is pulled by a horse in the same way as the carts of the milkman, the baker, the coalman and the greengrocer. They leave big heaps of manure on the road, which is prized by my Dad, who puts it into a sack and suspends it in the rainwater butt. He calls this his 'sock', and he uses it to make the tomatoes grow thick and lush, giving off that wonderful pungent peppery smell in the humid greenhouse that I love so much. The water is also boiled and used to wash my hair, so that must be why it grows so long and thick. The job of collecting the manure often falls to me; I am given the big shovel and told to follow the horse up the road. My embarrassment is intense as I try to lodge the elusive manure onto the shovel. It won't stay on, and always manages to plop back onto the road before it reaches the bucket. Huffing and sweating, pink with exertion, I struggle into the garden, trying hard not to be seen by anyone, and so avoid the taunts.

Growing up in the forties has its advantages. Cars are very few, and don't exist at all in the Street. I live in Paradise; that's what the area is called! There is a Crabmill Lane and an Eden Street, and an 'Adam and Eve' public house. Paradise is a world of red brick houses, dirty pavements, dusty entrys – and friendly helpful people. In the summer the small dark houses become hot and stuffy, so people sit on the front steps, calling to each other, chatting. My Mother 'doesn't' though, as she 'doesn't neighbour', and likes to keep herself to herself. She prefers to stay alone, sitting in the little back garden that is full of flowers. I love the garden; in the dark it becomes magical, as big white daisies turn into stars fallen from the night sky, and moths are fairies caught in moonbeams. The big dark expanse above me encircles my world. It closes around everything to keep it safe. When I discover that the roof to my world isn't really there at all, but an infinite void stretching beyond eternity, my horizons suddenly expand, but for now, I am content to walk up the uneven path and look at the white daisies, the pale pink rose on the wall, the Honeysuckle. I have my own little patch where I grow flowers from seeds. They grow into papery flowers that I hang up to dry in my Dad's shed, then I sell them back to my mother. In the kitchen I grow things too; I put carrot tops on a saucer in some water, then wait for the feathery green tops to sprout. Mustard and cress seeds are sprinkled onto damp blotting paper, then I have the little green tops in bread with cheese. Watching them grow from a small brown seed is a miracle I cannot fathom.

Dad has a small greenhouse where the tomatoes grow, their pungent smell clings to my fingers when I help him to take out the side shoots. This is a lovely job, the moist air in the greenhouse, and popping small tomatoes into my mouth when they are ripe. I have learned how to take cuttings from Dad's geraniums in August, popping them into the small trays and watching with wonder as they make roots and grow new leaves. This is my own little world; in the garden I know there are fairies, if I am still, I will see them. They only live in the garden, because in my bedroom, there are vampires, huge spiders, nasty whirling suns that press me down into the bed – but the garden is fairyland. In the daylight on sunny days, it is good to lie on my belly on the tiny patch of grass, and watch insects with iridescent wings scurrying about their affairs. If I lay

23

on my back I can watch the catkins and green leaves on the Silver Birch as the breeze moves them. Sometimes a dragonfly will skim over me and I dream I am sitting on his back, flying away to somewhere nicer than this. The sun catches his wings, turning them into rainbows. Ladybirds are gathered in a matchbox, counted, and released. Spiders are studied for long moments, as they spin their webs from leaf to leaf. My happiest hours are spent in the garden. Except on Mondays; Monday is washday, and it begins very early indeed.

On Monday, the fire beneath the brick copper in the corner of the kitchen is lit. All the clothes that have spent time soaking in the big tin bath are now loaded into the copper. This job begins at six o'clock in the morning, when Dad comes home from his night shift as Watchman from Courtaulds. In the top of the copper is a very big 'Dolly'. It looks like a cow's udder on a stick. There is also a copper stick, which I am afraid of. It is a very thick heavy stick used for poking the washing down, and also, sometimes to chastise me. Only when I have been particularly bad though. Washday is the worst day of the week. I am sat on the kitchen table and ordered not to move, and the ritual begins. Every article of clothing is washed according to its colour, rinsed in a bath of cold water, mangled in the enormous mangle that stands in the yard, into another bath of cold water, mangled again, then, pegged individually onto the line. Every sparkling white hankie is pegged neatly with its own wooden peg. The glutinous bowl of blue-white starch is on the kitchen table, and a 'Recketts' blue bag makes sure that her whites are perfect.

When the last article of clothing is blowing on the line, there is the copper to empty and clean, the mangle to dry, the tin bath to wipe out, the kitchen floor to scrub, the yard to be swilled down and swept. The brass hooks which are in the yard to hold the brooms are cleaned with Brasso until they gleam. The smell is steamy, like a suet pudding in the pan with its muslin cloth knotted tight. Little rivers of condensation run down the windows, which in their turn are leathered and buffed until they shine. Coming home on Mondays means that the back gate is locked until all is finished. The result is a gleaming yard and a tired, hot and cross Mother. Mondays are not my favourite day at all.

Chapter Five

There are lots of places I can go when I am in the way at home. Mrs Rawson likes me, she tells her sister. 'Such a nice polite little girl,' she says to Mrs Pollock. Mrs Rawson and Mrs Pollock live together. Though they are sisters, they are not alike at all. Mrs Rawson is a tiny bird-like woman who wears fine lacy cardigans and pearls around her thin neck. Her iron-grey hair is always in a tight little bun. Mrs Pollock is small, round and fat. Her face is stern and she has deep lines from her nose to her mouth. When she smiles, they disappear and move to her cheeks. A visit to the old ladies always means tea in a china cup and a special biscuit. It is difficult to balance my cup while I hold the saucer carefully and I find that my little finger pops up, just like my Dad's. I love to watch my Dad with a cup; He only has one arm, and the hand is rough and callused from years of hard work and gardening. Yet he holds his cup daintily, like a gentleman.

Mrs Rawson sits in an ancient leather chair filled with crochet cushions, the saucer balanced on her knee with a biscuit sitting in it, and the cup held very carefully. The sisters seem to have piles of books on every surface. Lots of books, lots of ornaments, and no space anywhere for a cup. The mantelpiece is decorated with a white lace cloth that has tassels hanging down. The clock that sits in the middle chimes every quarter hour. In the hearth there is a brass companion set, highly polished, a huge heavy poker and an even bigger bucket filled with coal. Either side of the clock there is a pottery dog. They both look the same, except they face each other. Dark brown linoleum covers the floor, which is highly polished just like the brass and the large table that sits in the middle of the room. A rag rug, just like the one at home, is the only cover for the linoleum, and it is very slippy. My mother pegs our rugs in the evenings, and I love sorting through all the bits cut ready to pull through the hessian. They are cut from our old clothes, and I can see my skirt, a winter coat or a dress as they take their place in the rug. Nothing is wasted.

Mrs Pollock and Mrs Rawson's cluttered room makes me feel comfortable, and I settle back, holding my cup carefully. Mrs Rawson sits on a high-backed chair, highly polished and with lovely big scrolls at the back. She rubs her tiny hands over the arms of her chair, feeling the wood, knobbly and smooth beneath her fingers. Her back is straight, the lace collar of her blouse lying flat and neat, a brooch pinned to the centre. Such a pretty brooch, with a big brown stone in it. It is from this position that Mrs Rawson talks to me. I am always careful not to talk about Mum or Dad because I have been warned. 'Never tell anyone your business,' that's what Mum says. 'Just be polite, but don't say anything about home.'

So I answer questions about school, and about Mr Coleman who teaches me piano. Mostly, I ask to look at the books. They have a lovely smell, like autumn leaves; as I carefully turn the pages, they rustle between my fingers. I love books, and Mrs Rawson seems to like me to look at them. Mrs Rawson has lost her husband in the War. This is what she tells me. On the mantelpiece by the dog there is a photo in a brass frame of a lady, young and very pretty, standing next to a tall stern man in a soldier's uniform. They look very serious. Mrs Rawson looks at it when she talks about her husband. Then her face softens, the corners of her mouth just tilting upwards as if she is going to smile. Her face becomes wistful again, and Mrs Pollock bustles in, her large bottom pulling at the chenille cloth, which is covering one half of the table. 'She doesn't want to hear all that Ethel' – 'Would you like another biscuit?' Politely I say, 'No thank-you', though really I would love another. They are covered in chocolate, not plain like the ones at home. 'Salome, give Dulcie another biscuit,' says Mrs Rawson, so I accept gratefully. Sometimes they just busy themselves with their chores, and leave me to read the books. The ones with pictures in are the best, as I cannot yet read so many words.. Looking at the pictures is wonderful, then I can tell myself the stories. Years later, I was to cross paths with Mrs Rawson again, but these times spent there as a small girl would always be treasured memories. The harsh realities of old age were still a long way away.

Chapter Six

Sylvia Faulkener's granny lives next door to Mr and Mrs Hadley, who come from Birmingham and they have a different way of talking to everyone else in the street. I listen closely, absorbing the rises and falls of their voices. At home in the kitchen, I mimic the nasal vowels to my mother. My sister, 12 years older than me, laughs in the musical way she has. 'Don't let them hear you our kid' – 'Don't encourage her...' This from the kitchen where Mum is cooking. Making them laugh feels good, but it's puzzling that I couldn't share it outside. Still, grown-ups are odd. When there is something really important I want them to hear, they don't even seem to know I am there. Then when I say something funny, I am told not to repeat it outside.

There are other ways of getting attention though. What about that lovely word I learned at the swing park up the 'Rec. 'Bloody' – that was it. I throw it into the silence around the kitchen table at teatime. It echoes, bouncing about in the silence which follows.

'Where did you get that from?'

'It's just a word,' I reply in my defence.

'Never say that again – it's a bad word.'

How can a word be bad? It's just lots of letters put together. 'What's wrong with bloody?'

Now, the air is tight. Dad is concentrating on chasing a

potato around his plate, not seeming to know what is happening. He always does that when issues have to be faced.

'Don't make such a fuss.' This from big brother, who usually spends his time teasing me to make me lose my temper. 'Our Dulc is a regular firebrand,' he says. Clive is ten years my senior. He is tall and very good-looking. I admire him from my small space, but remain in awe of him for many years.

Having got so much attention, I exploit the opportunity further. 'I can't see what's wrong with bloody, it only sounds like blood.' Now I am on dangerous ground. Mum sets her mouth into a downward arc, folds her arms, and issues the ultimate threat. *'Go to your room!'* she storms, and I know that no argument is expected. Defiance follows; making my way to the stairs, I turn back and say, 'I don't bloody care!' What a good way to be heard.

In my room now, I stare blankly over the rooftops. Shut up here again! The frustration and injustice scream in my head. The rooftops become blurred, seen through tears, which will not stop. I spend long hours up here; it is my mother's ultimate weapon when my questions become too many, my chattering too much, and my cheek too bold. *'Go to your room!'*

At first, I cry loudly, sobs hurting my chest. Eventually the tears dry up, so I force the sound of sobbing, so that they don't forget where I am. My hope is that my mother will come and give me a cuddle. But she doesn't come; I open the window, lean on the wooden sill, and I shout, 'I'm locked in up here!' – but no one listens, so I close the window again and sit on the bed. I am angry so I bang my fists on the door. I cry, forcing the tears and the sobs once more in the hope that somebody will listen.

Finally I give up and accept my fate, settle down to

wait. There are no toys up here, just a few precious books hidden under the bed with my torch, which I use for reading under the covers. My special book is called 'One hundred Fairy tales', given to me by Len, my sister's husband. It was his when he was young, and he reads from it sometimes at bedtime. The stories come to life for me then, and I can see the princesses, fairies and witches. I dance in the red shoes, and the stories follow me into my dreams. My bed is my place of fear, and I lie in the dark trying to stay on the edge, because I am sure there are hundreds of spiders crawling in the middle. I drift into uneasy sleep, and my dreams then come to haunt me. Now I am being pressed down by whirling suns, and vampires with hideous faces.

I wake shivering, to shrink from the spiders again. My window is locked to keep out the vampires, but they reach me when I sleep. There is a small picture on my wall of a galleon on big waves. The wall is painted pink and stippled, which makes the galleon look as if it sinking in the sickly pink water. Outside, it is raining, grey rain which colours everything grey. It washes down the roofs of the houses, runs into gutters, drips from the windowsill. Small drops trickle down the window- panes. I watch them fall, seeing tiny rainbows trapped within them. I look again at the galleon, close my eyes and see myself standing on its deck with the wind blowing in my hair. I can taste the salt water, feel it stinging my face. But it isn't the sea spray, only my tears. I watch a bird settle on the wet gutter. A quick shake of his feathers,, then he flies off into the grey sky. I wish I could do that, just spread my wings and fly. My room is cold, as the only warmth is from the coal fire in the downstairs grate. In the winter I run upstairs at bedtime clutching my hot water bottle, and bury myself into the soft covers.

I have a great fear of the dark; when my light is put out and the door closes, my room fills with indescribable horrors. I curl into a ball, keeping to the very edges of my bed, my limbs feeling swollen and heavy. Morning is a long time coming. When I wake up, the inside of my window is decorated with ice feathers curling into fantastic shapes. I push my fingers against them, making ridges of white ice. On these mornings I dash downstairs to the coal fire again. My Dad clears out the ash, and I wait until the sounds of the shovel and bucket stop before I go down. My clothes are warming in the hearth, so I watch the flames making glowing caverns filled with moving shapes and tiny dancing people. I have angry red patches on my legs where I get too close. The black kettle on its hob starts to whistle, and morning begins.

On Saturdays I sometimes go to the Slipper baths in Livingstone road. I pay my threepence, take my towel and little bar of soap, and go into a cubicle where I can lie in a big bath. It is always cold and the towel is rough to my skin, so I prefer the Saturdays when my Mother brings in the tin bath, filling it up with bowl after bowl of hot water. I am given the big jug to pour water over my hair and to wash off the lifebuoy soap. The big red soap is slimy and has a smell of disinfectant. It is used to wash my hair too, and then rinsed off with water from the outside water butt, which is warmed on the black range. The whole process takes a long time, and when I get out I am cold because the only warm space is facing the fire – an icy cold draught comes in through the sitting room door behind me. My environment is real; I feel it and experience its sensations. My imagination creates stories in my frost-laced window, worlds within the glowing embers of the fire. As an adult, I live in a centrally heated world, mov-

ing from heated home into heated car and then into over-
heated shops. The atmosphere is false, removed from reality. But for now, while I write, I live in a contrast of cold
and warm, a simpler existence where cause is effect, and
the results are instantaneous.

Chapter Seven

It is winter and the hedge at the bottom of our garden is bare, so I can watch Mr White and his pigs through the branches. I stand by the silver birch tree, hands pushed down into my pockets, fascinated by what I see. Mr White comes from London .He wears a bowler hat and a white silk scarf. His sleeves are always rolled up, and a cigarette dangles from his mouth. He uses really lovely words. Big, fat, long words that usually began with 'B', and are always said to the pigs. He lives at the back of the Street, and his muddy piece of ground is filled with old tumble-down sheds. The pigs live in these sheds. They are muddy and rout about in the mud all day, churning it into filthy heaps. I feel so sad for them as Mr White is always shouting at them, or hitting them with a stick.

'Why is he called Mr White, he should be Mr Black?' I ask.

'Stop asking silly questions,' is the only answer I get. Mum says he should be turned out. Our small back garden backs onto the pig ground, and rats sometimes scuttle through the top hedge and into our garden. Saturdays are often brightened up with Mum shouting, 'Sam!' or 'Clive! Fetch the rake, there's a rat in the garden.' Such a panic there is then; I can stand in the garden unseen by Mum and lost in the ensuing pandemonium as Clive or Dad charges to the hedge brandishing the rake. No one ever catches the rat, and I only see it twice. Maybe it is my mother's way of making everybody do things.

Sometimes, Mr White kills his pigs. Years later I am appalled by the barbarism of what I see, the horror of the act, but as a child, it is another thing to watch and to puzzle over. We try to protect children from horror, but it is the adult who is shocked – the child watches but doesn't absorb the reality of the deed. The pigs run and squeal, making the mud churn into a dark brown sea. Mr White, still wearing his black bowler hat, slits their throats, and I stand by the hedge watching. I am transfixed by the scene without taking in the cruelty. Mr White also has hens, and I watch as he twists their necks. They still run after he has taken their heads off. My sister pulls me away. 'Come on, Maybelle, you shouldn't be watching.' (Maybelle is my sisters' special name for me.) But I can't see why, because to a little girl of few years, it doesn't seem real.

Of all the people who live in the street, the ones to make the most lasting impression on me are the Bakers. The Bakers are the talk of the Street. My mother doesn't like me to go there, but I love them with a passion unexplainable. Their house is just two doors away from mine. It has a smell of dirty washing and stale cooking, but I don't mind at all. If I scratch my nail on the table or a chair arm, it is filled with black grease... the mat and cushion covers are frayed and threadbare, and the Bakers shout a lot. It doesn't seem to mean anything, their shouting. They laugh when they shout, and they use lovely words. I am now becoming wise. When I am in the Bakers', I never tell. I also never repeat the words, but save them, wrap them up in my mind for when I play games in the street with the others.

It is very strange how Mum always seem to know when I have been there. 'You've been to the Bakers' again,' she accuses. How does she know? Another mystery I have to solve. So I play outside for a while before I go in again. Old Mrs Baker is small; her hair is short and grey, and has yellow streaks. It sticks out from the side of her head in unruly spikes. She wears a pinafore that crosses over at the back and is covered with black marks down each side where she wipes her hands. Her son Bill seems too old to be her son. He is a huge man with a red face and a deep loud voice. He lifts me up with enormous red rough hands, and sets me gently down again, and I am never afraid of him. Sometimes he comes in smelling the same as the Red House pub. Then, he is very happy and talks even louder than usual. Mum says that he is not quite right, but I am not sure what she means – he seems very right to me. So many things are said in my presence because I am invisible. I move secretly within my invisibility with ease. It feels comfortable, and makes no demands on me.

Daisy comes to live with the Bakers, and I like her too. Bill marries Daisy and the whole Street is talking about it. Daisy is 'not nice'. She has shared a house with Asians who lived up the road and people said she was a 'pro', though I don't know what that means. This makes no difference to my visits, though I don't tell my mother when I go. This is easy, as she never asks where I am. Daisy and Bill have a baby, and I sit watching it, tiny fists waving and its face all red and screwed up. This is new to me, as we haven't any babies at our house.

There is another baby up the street called Johnnie Daleman, and sometimes I walk the pram up and down with Sylvia and Roy Faulkener, but I never see him out of the pram. Daisy has a cross face, her mouth turns down at the corners and her voice is harsh. She always has a cigarette in her mouth, which makes her talk sideways, but not when she holds the baby. Then, her voice is soft and she smiles. The day that Daisy's mother comes to visit her creates great talk over the back fences as women hang out their washing. Her mother arrives in a car, an unknown thing in the Street. There are only bikes in the Street, so we all stand and look. Curtains move and shadowy faces peer out. One or two, who don't mind being seen like Mrs Miller, come onto their front steps to watch. My mother, far too dignified to join in street gossip, stays in her back parlour out of sight. The events in the Street do not interest her.

Daisy's mother speaks with a very posh voice and wears a dead animal wrapped around her neck. It seems a very funny thing to do as it even has eyes. How terrible, to have eyes around your neck, and the smell of dead animal next to your nose. At tea-time I listen as my mother tells my father about the incident, and how she feels sorry for Daisy's mother. Daisy has gone astray, and her mother must feel very ashamed.

'What is "gone astray"?' I ask.

The question is answered, as is every question, with the reply, 'You are just like Tennyson's babbling brook, you go on forever.'

Now there is another question. 'What is Tennyson's babbling brook?' Silence follows that one, as the adults continue with their conversation, leaving me invisible again.

Vera also lives at the Bakers'; she is married to Jack and they have a little boy named Jackie. Vera is my favourite, she is enormously fat and very smelly, but she laughs a lot and always listens to my chattering. Vera takes me to see her friend who has a baby. Ann lives in a tiny back bedroom in a big dirty old house on the Stoney Stanton Road. To reach her room we have to go through a dark empty room where a push-bike leans on a wall with peeling brown wallpaper, and up steep wooden stairs that have no light. Ann is sitting behind a wooden airer filled with wet napkins. They are drying round an old gas fire, which splutters and turns the flames blue. The feelings of hopelessness and poverty I absorb on this visit stay with me throughout my life. This is a place I never want to be in.

Vera and Ann talk to each other, they seem at home in the surroundings that distress me so much. They laugh a lot, and I know somehow that these things are not to be repeated. If I keep quiet, they will forget me, and I will learn more. This is interesting – this is sex education, and all the little whispered remarks are followed by loud laughter. They don't mean much, but I store away the whispers like a treasure, to discuss with friends in the playground when I need something to bargain with later.

Vera takes me with her to many things, and my mother doesn't seem to mind as long as I am out of the way and not talking. Today, we are going to a wedding. I have never been to a wedding before so I am excited. My mother isn't very happy about this trip, but I finally get the needed permission on the understanding that I stay with Vera. The big room is very full of people; they are drinking, eating and all talking at once. I am disappointed because I think that brides wear long white dresses, but all she has is a bunch of flowers, which she throws onto the table and leaves. The people get noisier and noisier and I stand in my best blue coat and watch. I watch a lot, and they forget that I am there at all. I am always a watcher, an observer as life flows around me. I float behind an invisible screen of anonymity.

The wedding is such an occasion. Vera's husband Jack has started to fall about. He can't stay standing and Vera is shouting at him. 'Not in front of her,' she says, pointing to me. Then a lady gets onto a table where all the plates have been stacked, and all the men, especially Jack, are cheering. She starts to take off her clothes as they all clap. Vera is laughing, so is everyone else. The lady has taken off her dress and is now just in her underwear. I begin to cry quietly; this isn't right, and I am afraid. Taking off your clothes when people are looking is really bad.

Vera grabs my hand and says to Jack, 'I'm taking her home.'

"S'all right, it won't hurt her,' Jack slurs and falls, dribbling down his shirt. Vera pushes him away; she is bigger than him, so he falls over easily. Pulling me away, Vera takes me home, pushing my head into her soft warm chest, and wiping my tears away.

The story of the wedding stays hidden in the storehouse of my memory, too shameful to be repeated, for many years. I often think about it though, because if this is what being grown-up and having a husband means, then I am afraid to grow up. My dad isn't like that. He is very quiet and does what Mum tells him to. Or he goes to his allotment and comes home smelling of peppermints. His allotment is a good place to go to, but he doesn't always take me with him. These are the days when he is a long time and smells of peppermints. Sometimes I go with my Dad to his allotment and help him to water. The canal runs alongside the little plots of land, so I take a big old saucepan and stoop down to the edge of the canal, filling the pan with water, feeling very important. There is a shed on his allotment where he keeps his tools, and I like to go in there on cold days to wait for him.

'Dad, what's this little hole for?' I push my fingers through the hole and wait for an answer.

Dad smiles and says, 'That's for when I'm took short.'

'What's took short, Dad?' He smiles again, but doesn't answer, so I go and refill the saucepan, not satisfied with my answer, but at least it was an answer.

Going to the pictures is forbidden at home because it is against God's word, but I sometimes creep off with the others on a Saturday morning, joining the threepenny rush for the 'bug and flea hole' – the local cinema. Today, we join the queue outside the Prince of Wales, pushing and shoving; we sit down in the dark cinema on the scratchy plush seats. The film breaks down, so we stamp our feet and shout 'Why are we waiting?' very loudly.

Now it is over, and we spill out onto the pavement from the darkness to make our way home. It is raining, and there is a heavy black cloud in the sky. I begin to run, but the black cloud is following me – getting blacker and lower. Now there is the roar of thunder, and I am terrified. This must be the wrath of God; he has seen me go to the pictures, and now I am going to be punished. I run faster, but the cloud stays with me, and the thunder gets louder still. I arrive home, wet and frightened, to tell my mother where I have been. The fear of this stern God is greater than the fear of my mother's anger. 'He sees everything you do,' I am told. I wonder if he sees me in the outside lavatory, or when I pick my nose.

Vera wants to take me to the cinema – not the 'bug and flea' hole, but a cinema called the Roxy that is a long way away on the Foleshill Road. My mother has agreed that I can go, but I am not sure why God will let me go with Vera. Maybe Mum has asked him and it is alright this once. The trip to the cinema with Vera will be special. It is to see Mario Lanza in 'The Great Caruso'. We enter the dark cinema and sit down at the back in the plush seats. Now I enter a magical world of music, which is different from anything I have ever seen or heard. This is a major discovery and it so beautiful that I cry. All those sounds, like drops of gold and silver, I feel them fall about me and I want so much to catch them. I walk home in a dream, unaware of the dark, the hard dirty pavements. I am floating home on a wave of music. Vera laughs at me but it is kind laughter, and I don't mind. Mum, Dad, Myrtle, they all laugh at me. Their laughter isn't always kind, as they laugh when I drop things or ask questions.

'Our kid is so clumsy,' my sister says, so I get nervous and drop something else.

Why will no one ever listen and answer my questions? I have so many of them. Every day my life presents me with more.

At the Bakers' house they now have a dog, and I love to bury my face into her fur, smell her and feel the warmth of her smooth brown body. I love animals, and stroke all the cats and dogs in the street. My father loves them too, but Mum says they are dirty and she won't have them. Dad has a little ginger cat in his time office at work. He walks home each morning along the Foleshill road and down Broad Street, with Ginger wrapped around his neck. When he goes again at night, Ginger jumps onto his back and sits there again, all the way to Courtaulds. My mother allows Ginger to be in the house this time for some reason I cannot work out.

There are so many inconsistencies in my mother's rules. It seems to me that she can make then suit any situation, but the contradictions are a puzzle for a small girl. Dad plays with the cat at work, chasing him around the yard. He tells me how Ginger hides, then jumps out on him. Then one day Dad comes home sad, without Ginger, because Dad had opened the big gates for a lorry and Ginger thought he was playing. He ran out to hide and the lorry ran over him.

So I make do with other people's animals, until the day that the Bakers' dog has puppies. What a miracle! All those tiny wriggling bodies, eyes tight-shut, burrowing into the mothers' tummy and sucking with great big slapping sucks. Every day I run round and sit watching them. Nobody seems to mind me being there, talking to the puppies. Now, the Bakers' house smells of warm puppies. I like it, but have to wash when I go home again, because of germs. The day has come when the puppies can leave their mother; Bill places a small snuffly bundle of brown fur into my arms. 'Go and ask your Mum if you can have him.'

I run down the entry clutching the puppy. Dad is in his shed tidying screws and escaping from Mum. He takes the puppy, holds it, talks to it, then says, 'Her won't let you keep un.' With the confidence of the young and the eternal belief that people will be alright in the end, I face my mother.

If I had taken in a tiger the reaction couldn't have been any worse. Mother draws herself up, folds her arms, and assumes the expression that always brings fear and rebellion bubbling up inside me.

FROM PARADISE TO EDEN

'Take it out! *Now!*'

Further discussion is impossible, so with tears dropping onto the puppy's face, watched sadly by Dad, I take the little animal back. I am so sad, and so angry. It isn't very much to want, just a dog of my own. I am silent, my resentment smouldering like a neglected fire; it burns slowly beneath its surface of acceptance.

Doreen Luckett's gran has a dog. Only it isn't alive any more. It had been – once. Now, its head is mounted over the sitting room door. I stand looking at it, mesmerised by the glassy eyes that see nothing and I wonder how they did it. Did the dog die first? What did they fill his head with? Grandmother's dog fills my night-time terrors for many months to come, the sightless stare looming into the darkness of my room to haunt me.

Doreen's granddad works at Lissaman's Bakery, so we walk there together through the narrow entries and stand at the bake-house door. Her granddad brings us each a neatly folded cone of greaseproof paper filled with confectioner's cream. We rip the end of the cone away with our teeth, and slowly squeeze the cream into our mouths. The taste of the cream and the hot crusty smell of the bakery are a delight. Sometimes, there are buns covered in burnt sugar, which we tuck into our pockets and take to our hiding place on the 'bombie'. Here we have made a secret place in a hole where a bomb fell. We have lined it with twigs and left some to pull over the entrance. It is where we share secrets and take treats to savour.

We are Coventry back street children, emerging from the Second World War, and we run in our street without much restriction. There has been too much confining, in air-raid shelters and glory holes. Sometimes we squabble and fight, and not just the boys are aggressive. Doreen is my best friend, but we fall out, and there I am, that sweet little girl so loved by Mrs Rawson, and I am swinging Doreen around by her plaits. She is bigger than I am, but I am very angry and I swing her hard as she shouts. The others stand and cheer me on, but it is soon over, and play begins again. I am not always victorious though. There is a morning when I go to call for Doreen at her gran's' house, and she shouts out that she doesn't want to play with me. I stand and call her for a very long time, before going home and crying bitterly in our front room.

We pass time away by swinging on the bus-pole. Some girls can swing right round, but I hate the feel of falling, so I just watch with envy.

Death is a mystery that becomes just a part of living as I grow up. I have watched Mr White's pigs and hens die, and death is talked about at home. I know that people have died in the war, that plants die to be born again when seeds germinate. Still, one thing haunts me as a small girl. A girl in the Street, who is more Clive's age than mine, is very ill, and she lies in her bed in the small front room. I go to see her, hesitant, in awe of something beyond my understanding. I am told that she is dying, but all I can see is a girl, yellow-white like wax. She lies in her bed silently, and sadness hangs around her so heavy that I feel I can touch it. I can smell 'death'.

As children growing up in this time, death becomes just another part of living. It isn't sanitised or removed neatly from sight, not the way it will be in the future. So we accept it, come to terms with it. It is real.

The Street is our playground, where we run to escape from the confines of back yards. The games are many and numerous, our imaginations creating worlds forever new. Shadows, or Statues, tests our ability to be still, and is the most popular game of all. One person stands on the pavement, back turned, while the others stand on the opposite pavement. The object is to get to the other side without being seen to move.

This means stopping in funny positions every time the person who is 'on' turns round, and there is a lot of argument involved.

'You moved!'

'No I didn't!'

'She did, I saw her.' The game is abandoned for skipping.

Skipping is supposed to be for the girls, but the boys join in, pushing and shouting until we send them away. They go off to shoot each other with sticks of wood, or to play marbles in the gutter. They call it 'allies', and it becomes very competitive. We skip with lengths of clothesline cadged from willing mothers. An extra long piece is good, as then we can all join in. We stand at either end to turn the rope, and the others jump in as we chant:

'Mrs M, Mrs I, Mrs SSI, Mrs S, Mrs SIPPI.'

The next chant is always 'All in together girls, this fine weather girls', and finishes with 'O-U-T spells *out!*' This we continue until there is no one left to jump in. There is quite a skill in jumping in, and the rope stings my legs when I miss. The boys stand and jeer at these chants, before punching each other or running off to other diversions. Then the skipping stops while we chase the boys.

'The farmer's in his den 'is my least favourite game. It finishes with the girl in the middle having to kiss the boy, and that is horrible. Terry Savage always smells of sausages, and he makes grabs at my dress when I run. Some of the girls love it and try to get into the middle, but I hang back and try to avoid it. Games of hide and seek, or treasure hunt are played in the entries which run at the back of the little terraced houses. As the gates are usually open or hanging off their hinges, it makes the tiny gardens good for hiding in. Some of the gardens are neat and pretty, like mine. My mother and father love their garden, but our gate is locked with a high trellis around it. No one is welcome to run into our garden.

The maze of entries, linking Bryn Road to Silverton Road and Crabmill lane are our extended playground. Dustbins spill over their rubbish, dogs forage in the spilt papers, and dog mess is to be avoided if possible. Going home for dinner with dog mess on my shoes is not good. 'You've trodden in business again our Dulcie', take your shoes outside and scrub them'. The back of Chippie Kilburns is the best; it has a nose clogging smell of rotten fish, and old chip papers blow along it, wrapping around my legs. The local chip shop is where in later years, we hang about to meet the boys, but now it is a good narrow entry to run and chase through, hiding behind the dustbins, then running and scattering dustbin lids with loud clanging. The shouts of Chippie Kilburn telling us to 'B****** off!' adds to the fun. Knocking off dustbin lids is just another diversion, our progress along the entries tracked by the shouts of 'Bloody kids'! The summer holidays from school are very long, so when we tire of street games, we go along Crabmill Lane to the 'cut' which is what we call the canal. There is an old tree hanging over the water on which we have tied a piece of rope. Then, the braver ones amongst us hold onto the rope and swing out over the water. Sometimes someone will fall in, but they just swim to the bank and we all laugh. It doesn't stop us from the swinging.

Oscar Bradshaw lives by Chippie Kilburns, and his mum owns the shop where my dad buys his electrical stuff. They have wireless sets in the dusty window with knobs, which should be shiny but are always covered in dust. Oscar tries to join in the entry games, but we chant to him with the cruelty of childhood 'Oscar's fat and that is that'. He perseveres and wins in the end, joining in the chase and finding someone else to taunt. The jungle world of city street children in the 1940s is harsh but usually fair. Oscar's clothes are always nice with no holes or missing buttons, and in the winter he always has gloves *and* a scarf. My gloves are knitted by my mother, with a crocheted cord passing through each sleeve. This is because I always lose them.

Mrs Bradshaw rides a very old bike, which creaks as she peddles it along. She is very, very fat, and her bottom hangs over the saddle so that it doesn't seem to have a saddle at all. We all run at a reasonable distance behind her, giggling, and diving into entries when she turns round. Mr Bradshaw is very small, so they look very funny to us when they go out together.

The pavements are very good for games, especially Hopscotch and Leapfrog. Someone brings a piece of chalk, and numbers are chalked onto the paving slabs. We push and jostle for our turn and coats are dropped onto the floor as we get hotter.

Someone shouts 'Come on!' – we all follow, and our progress up the street is followed by the angry shouts from front doors. This is 'Rat-Tat-Ginger', we knock the doors and run into the entries, as cries of 'I'll tell your mother, I know who you are' fall on deaf ears.

I like being outside, because being inside means being quiet while my mother has 'forty winks', or does Bible readings. Outside, I feel free because if I am out of sight, no one worries about what I am doing. On these occasions I play alone when no one else is out. I draw chalk numbers on the pavement outside my house, and also on Mr Wilkins' house next door. Today, old Mr Wilkins comes out and shouts at me. He stands on his step, glasses sliding down his nose and his black shiny waistcoat stretching over a fat stomach. As he shouts, a big watch in his pocket bounces like his glasses. I run into the kitchen crying, and there is my Dad, my champion. Usually gentle and mild tempered, he bristles with unaccustomed anger. His stump, which is all there is left of his right arm, quivers with indignation. I follow him out, standing back a little way to avoid any backlash, as he bangs on Mr Wilkin's door. The loud argument that follows is witnessed by half the Street. They come to their steps wiping their wet hands on already soiled pinafores, whispering behind their hands, ' Its her again, what's she been up to now?' The excitement is short-lived, and my Dad goes back into the kitchen to a tongue lashing from my mother. He is glowing! It is worth it, just to say what he feels for once.

Chapter Eight

There is always traffic of some sort in the Street. Horses and carts mostly, but bikes are the biggest hazard, especially when Alfred Herberts factory comes out at dinnertime. Then, the bikes flood the street, all going in one direction. Being called in for my dinner, and knowing I must respond immediately, I take chances. Anything is better than my mother's impatience. I run for it, letting the bikes swerve around me. The men swear at me 'You silly little bugger', but the risk is worth it all, as my mother's anger is much more difficult to handle.

Today, I misjudge my run, and I come a cropper. Bowled over by one bike, I am then run over by lots of others who haven't seen me, or couldn't stop in time. I don't tell my mother why my knees are bloodied and my dress ripped. So much easier to let her think I have been playing rough than to admit to bike dodging. Life is always a case of which 'truth' will carry the least punishment. Playing rough is understood by my mother, and is often the cause of punishment. I have a lovely blue silk dress, made for me by mum and embroidered with bunches of flowers. It is Sunday, so I am dressed in blue and sent out to play, with instructions to 'Stay clean'! There is a lovely big puddle of black stuff in the road, so I poke it, then wipe my fingers down my dress. Seeing the black marks, I try to hide in the pantry where our sink is. I must rub it off before she sees it… It won't budge, and I am in such trouble. I have been playing in tar!

Our vegetables are grown by my Dad on his allotment, but we sometimes have Eddy the 'Veg man' to bring them on his cart. His day is Friday, so we all wait for him on the street corner. He is a nice man who loves us all, and he has lovely fair wavy hair. He turns his horse and cart into our street, loaded with fruit and vegetables and huge sacks of potatoes. There is a space by his side, and the quickest child is hoisted up and taken with him on his rounds. We hop off, and run up the entries, banging on the back doors, which is great for Eddy, as all he does is sit on the cart until everyone comes out. Eddy brings the cart round for old Mrs Smith who keeps the greengrocer's shop on the Stoney Stanton Road. There are always dead birds and rabbits hanging in a row outside, their stomachs slit open. Mrs Smith is tiny with very short straight white hair that sticks out from beneath a tattered black felt hat. She hasn't got any teeth, so that when she smiles, which she does a lot, her lips vanish into her mouth. She always wears a coat that has no sleeves on top of her frock, and a belt around her waist with a money bag on it.

When Eddy pulls the cart into our Street, Mrs Miller is usually first out, her pinafore crossed over and tied at the back, just like my mothers. Mrs Miller is respected because her husband cleans the windows. He comes to each house along the street, propping his ladder against the bedroom window and hanging his bucket on the top, and if I stand underneath, I am splashed with water

Today the sweep is coming, and this is a very big occasion. The day begins very early, when the sheets are taken from Dads' shed and carefully draped over the sofa and the chairs, the table, the grandmother clock and the wireless which sits on a shelf next to the Bible. This takes a long time, making my mother all hot and bothered. She tells me she is 'meithered', and that I am meithering her This last word is always used when I am in the way. 'Go out and play, you're meithering me'. What is 'meithering'? – which usually turns out to mean I am a nuisance. So I wait at the top of the entry until I see Mr Fitter the Sweep coming round the corner pushing his handcart. There are lots of brushes, which stick out from beneath a dirty cloth. Mr Fitter has a black face, which is streaked with little rivers of sweat, leaving pale patches on his cheeks. His cap is covered in soot, as is his coat, hands and shoes. I watch, and wonder if Mr Fitter is always that colour, or maybe he is a different colour on Sundays. Does Mrs Fitter allow him in the house like that? When he smiles it is a surprise as his teeth and big pink gums look frightening. He is quite nice, and though I am not allowed in while he pushes the brushes up the chimney, I can watch from outside and shout loudly when the brush appears, poking out of the stack.

After Mr Fitter has trundled off with his cart, Dad gathers all the soot into an old cloth and carries it off to his Allotment. He comes back as black as Mr Fitter, and has to swill it off in the water butt before he is allowed to come in. Then, the cleaning begins; the paint-work is washed down, curtains are removed and put into the old stone copper in the corner of the kitchen, and furniture is polished until it gleams. This is my time to disappear before being accused of meithering again.

We spend a lot of time playing on the Bombies, which are the areas of piled up bricks and deep craters where houses had once been. They make good places too, for Dens and for holding concerts. In Crabmill Lane there is a very big crater which has become our theatre, so we take it in turns to stand on the high edge and sing, recite or dance. We hang around on the bombsites, just loitering, kicking brick-ends and idly chasing each other. It is winter and our feet get cold and wet as we push them through layers of dirty slushy snow. The damp seeps into our toes but somehow it doesn't matter. We are out and we are free and that feels good. The piles of rubble left over from bombed houses make good places to hide in, and games are invented, our minds ever reaching to new levels. 'Necessity is the mother in invention' – that's what my mum says. She has lots of sayings, one to fit every occasion.

It is Bonfire Night, and for weeks we have been gathering rubbish from gardens and Allotments, hauling it all to the bombie where a huge bonfire is beginning to grow. Grown-ups bring their rubbish, and make it grow even bigger. Some of the children have fireworks, so it doesn't matter that I haven't got any, I watch the others. Boys have jumping jacks, which I hate. They let them off behind us, and we run screaming into the entries, which makes the boys laugh. The Catherine Wheels spin round on their pins, sending lots of shining sparks shooting off into the darkness, spinning for a long time.

The darkness isn't a problem; this small world in which we live is a safe one where fear doesn't lurk. We run behind each other through the entries, shouting and dodging jumping jacks. Sid owns the shop at the top of the Street, where I always take my threepence on Saturdays. He sells lots of lovely sweets, gob-stoppers and liquorice wood. This is a special night, so Sid puts lots of long tables in the street, then with the help of his wife Ruby, he gives sausage and mash to us all. We push each other for first turn, but all get served in the end. We fetch big potatoes from our kitchens and poke them into the edges of the fire, which is now glowing red. Then we haul them out again with sticks, split them open and eat them. No one seems to get burnt and no one tells us to be careful. We know the dangers of the fire – we are street-wise kids.

Now Johnny Richards, helped by his brother Gus, drags his piano into the street and plays. This is wonderful, and I know that I want to play like this too. Johnny plays in a band, so he is very good. He has never had any lessons, but plays by ear, my Dad says. We dance around the piano and sing loudly, the grown-ups singing songs I don't know, but which stay in my memory so that I still remember all the words years later. I love Bonfire Night, and always manage to find a place just by the piano, watching Johnny's fingers racing up and down the keyboard. I watch Johnnie Richards walking up the street with his little dog on the end of a piece of string. The dog goes everywhere with him; I wonder whether it goes with him in the evenings when he plays in the band.

I play the piano too; our piano is in the front room, which we only use at Christmas, but I am allowed to play the piano in it. Mr Coleman from over the road has taught me to read music, though I spend hours making up my own tunes. My piano is important to me, and my sister Myrtle plays it too. She plays a song called 'The old fiddler' and it makes me cry, which makes her laugh. I teach myself to read lots of music, and when I am feeling very sad or lonely, this is where I go, letting the music wrap around me. I cannot imagine ever being without the piano.

Sunday morning is here, so we stand at the corner of the street and wait for the Salvation Army band. We can hear it playing as it comes along Eden Street and on to the Stoney Stanton road, so we quickly grab pennies and we wait. It comes into view, so we all run to join on the end, and we march – our arms swinging back and forth. They stop on the corner of Silverton Road, and we stay to listen. Sunday mornings mean roast meat, Billy Cotton on the wireless, the Salvation Army band – and forty winks. I can smell forty winks; it smells of roast lamb and apple tart, and mothballs. My mother's Sunday coat smells of mothballs. When it is time, after the dinner plates have been washed and dried in the pantry, my mother settles down in her chair and closes her eyes. Forty winks is a blanket of boredom and silence.

Bible readings are another form of torture to be endured, the safest place being under the heavy oak table. A gold chenille cover hangs over its edges making it dark and secret. My mother and father each read a passage from the bible in turn. Now it is Dad's turn, and I hold my breath. He grew up in the countryside near Oxford in a little village long since gone called Grimsbury. One of a large family and a tired mother, his schooling was not a priority. He begins to read...

'And there were 'arpers 'arping on their 'arps,' he reads.

He pauses; my mother breathes hard in her authoritative voice: '*Sam*! It's "And there were harpers harping on their harps"! 'There are aitches there!'

Poor Dad! And yet he endures these nightly readings patiently, as he does everything in his life. He manages to avoid most of the confrontations between me and my mother, though these are many and often. She is not listening to me again, and I have so much to tell her. Why won't she listen? I beat my fists on her legs, pull her pinafore, but she just stares distractedly through the window and says 'Mmmm...' I get angry, throwing myself on the floor, and she notices me. Today I am very angry, so my dad is called. They turn on the cold tap at the stone sink in the pantry and hold my head under it. Dad isn't happy and helps unwillingly. Later, he sits me on the floor between his legs and gently rubs my long hair until it is dry.

Our back bedroom is a good place to go to on wet days, or days when I am in the way. My dad has brought me home an old gramophone with a handle to wind it up. He has also given me some records. I have Paul Robeson singing 'My curly headed babby' and 'The moonlight sonata'. There is also 'The thunder and lightning polka' and a record of Snow White singing 'One day my prince will come' in a high wobbly voice. An old battered tin trunk is in here and it is full of wonderful clothes. They have been given to my mother by Mrs Critchley, a lady from 'The meeting'. There is a blue dress with points on the bottom, and a red velvet dress trimmed with black lace. I put them on, play the records, and I dance. Now, I am on the stage, people are clapping as I turn and bend my arms. The door suddenly bursts open, and I am humiliated as my mother and my sister fall in, laughing. Red colour creeps into my cheeks as I run down the stairs to my safe place under the table.

This must be a special occasion because Doreen Luckett is allowed to come into the back bedroom to play – yet another of my mother's inconsistencies. We dress up, tucking our dresses into our knickers and pushing sticks down the side for swords. Then we dance to the gramophone music while my Mum and sister watch. This time they laugh nicely and they clap. My mother has tears running down her face as they watch us. Doreen pulls out her sword and it gets stuck in her knicker elastic, which makes them laugh even more.

The Stoney Stanton Road is busy, I mustn't go across on my own, but if Audrey Crutchlow wants to play with me, I am taken over by my mother. Audrey's father owns the garage so they have lots of nice things. We play on the concrete by the pumps and it smells of petrol. Because my shoes get dirty, they have to be taken off when I go home. Audrey has a weak heart my mum says, so I have to be very careful when I play with her. No rough games or running. She is very pretty and looks delicate, and I am really careful with the self-importance of responsibility. I am the only girl who is asked to go and play, so I feel very honoured and, somehow special.

Mrs Pollock and Mrs Rawson have a niece who lives in Kenilworth, which is a very posh place to live. I have never been, but today I am being collected in a car by their niece, and taken to play with her little girl who is called Angela. They want me to go because they say I am a nice well- mannered little girl, so I am warned by my mother to remember my manners. The car arrives, a big black one, and I am very excited as I climb into the big back seat. Angela's mother is talking to me, but I cannot answer. 'Have you lost your tongue?' she asks me. I haven't lost my tongue, but I have only ever been in a car once before, and I am too excited to speak.

The house in Kenilworth is like nothing I have seen before, with its long back garden full of trees. The living room is so lovely; it has a polished table with flowers in a vase. Everything shines; copper buckets, brass dogs and small glass ornaments are in the hearth and on the mantelpiece. It is Christmas, and there is an enormous tree in the room hung with glass figures and draped with tinsel. This is like fairyland, and I wish that we had things like this. We don't have a Christmas tree at home. When I get home again, I get out the duster and polish our big table, telling my mother about Angela's house and how it's all shiny. My mother is hurt, and I don't understand why until many years later. Our house is always clean and nice, but not like Angela's.

Chapter Nine

I have a new bike, my very first, bought for me because I have passed the 11-plus and got a scholarship to Stoke Park Grammar school. Dad takes me down to the ' black pad' every night, he runs with me while he holds the saddle of my bike with his one arm. I can feel the air whistle past my ears and it feels free, exciting. Dad says, 'I have let go, you're on your own' – and I promptly fall off. This happens every evening for almost a year before I finally believe that I can do it. His patience, as always, never fails.

I am getting older – bike rides can now go beyond the Street. Doreen Luckett brings her bike, and I have my shiny new one. We feel very grown up as we head off towards Henley Road. Out of breath, we get off and push for a while, stopping occasionally to pull up socks or tie hair back. There is a van parked in front of us that we take little notice of, until the man gets out and stands behind it. We watch him as he undoes the zip on his trousers, and we are no longer curious, just very frightened. We see what we have never seen before, and we run, too afraid to get onto our bikes, we just run and run, arriving home out of breath. We never tell our parents, it remains a secret from them because we know instinctively that future trips will be forbidden, but we repeat the story with relish and embellishment in the street and the playground.

It is a sunny evening in late summer when we set off again for a bike ride. This time we head for Crackley woods, me first because I am sure I know how to get there. We dawdle, race down hills, stop to pick flowers, but Crackley woods seems no nearer, and now, we don't know where we are. Doreen starts crying, she is worried and frightened, so I take charge. This is an adventure and I am not afraid. It is getting darker now; the sun has gone leaving a red stain in the sky. We try to find our way, Doreen is really upset, so I go to a little police station and ask for help. We are in a little village named Wolvey. I tell them that my Dad is a works policeman at Courtaulds, and they ring him up. Dad is very cautious, not believing that it is me. He thinks that someone is trying to lure him away from his post. I convince him at last, and a van arrives to take us and our bikes home. It is now very late and very dark, and I am in big trouble. This feels so unjust, as it was my taking charge that got us home and I feel that I should be praised. After this escapade I am stopped from big bike rides for some time to come.

Dad has a bike that he sometimes uses for going to work. My friend Jean Arnold has come for me, and we all set off on our bikes, me, Dad and Jean. We arrive at the Memorial Park, and ride along the Kenilworth Road to the Spinney. I need to go to the toilet, so Dad tells me to go behind the trees. This I do, but lose my balance and fall, sitting in a large bed of stinging nettles. My yells call my dad over, and his solution is to line my knickers with dock leaves. I have a very uncomfortable ride home, and a spectacular red rash on my bottom.

There is excitement in our Street today, so I join the other kids to watch, not understanding what is happening, but caught up in the atmosphere. A woman is at Mrs

Applewaite's door, and Mrs Applewaite is shouting at her. Then Mrs Applewaite begins to hit the woman, shouting even louder. The woman runs off, and then Mr Applewaite is there and Mrs Applewaite is hitting *him* and shouting again. Seeing grown-ups acting like this is confusing, yet somehow there is comfort in it too. Maybe Mrs Applewaite will have her head put under the cold tap too. Later, I hear my mother and father talking about it all, and Mum says that Mr Applewaite was 'having another woman', so Mrs Applewaite sorted them out. It all seems to settle down though, and I see Mr and Mrs Applewaite going out together arm in arm.

The Street is a world; there is no world beyond this until I am 11 years old. It is complete within itself, a living breathing community with its tragedies, and its humour. It is a separate universe with diverse richness of characters, which is both safe and claustrophobic, inviting both the need to escape and the fear of leaving.

Life is not without its calamities, and I am a forgetful child. There are so many things happening inside my head, I find the outside world a difficult one to inhabit. Going to the Co-op for bread is a job I like, because I can pick off the burnt crust and eat it on my way home. I seem to get away with this most of the time, the damaged bread just put into the big enamel bread-bin in the pantry. To-day I have a small silver sixpence in my hand, my job is to collect the bread. I run along the pavement kicking stones and looking in the window of Bradshaw's electrical shop. My sixpence falls from my hand, and it rolls into the gutter, down the drain.

What now? I sit on the kerb by the drain, staring into the filthy depths. How can I go home and tell my mother that I have lost the sixpence? I am afraid of her anger; she is always telling me that we are very short of money, that she only has enough from Dad's weekly pay packet to put away the rent, the electric, the gas and the insurance. It doesn't leave enough for extras, and without the allotment we would struggle to eat. This is why she gets bones from the butcher, so that she can stew them with the vegetables and feed us. Every Friday Dad hands over his pay packet, and the contents are spread out on the old oak table. My mother's wooden box is brought out, and the envelopes inside are placed on the table. She carefully shares the money between envelopes, putting some in her purse, giving some to my father and then handing over my sixpence. The box is then put back into its hiding place under the stairs, though it is taken up to bed with her every night. Now I have lost sixpence, and she is going to be angry again. I am a stupid, careless silly little girl who can't be trusted to do anything.

I sit on the pavement and cry, feeling very sorry for myself. Mr Threadgold who lives next to the Greengrocer's shop comes to see why I am crying. Mr Threadgold has no legs, and sits on the step in his wheelchair. He gives me another sixpence, and I am so pleased that I say 'thank you' over and over again. Now I can go and get the bread and my mother will never know that I have been stupid again.

My forgetfulness is not always so easily solved though, and sometimes I am in much more trouble. I have been sent to the Co-op with money in an envelope to get the milk checks. My sister has sent me this time because my mother is in hospital and she is looking after me. She also gives me a letter to post, so I run round to the Paradise post office with the letter and the envelope in my hand. I am thinking about the story read to me by Len. It's about a princess who sleeps on a bed with a pea under the mattress. I push the letter into the pillar-box, listening for it to drop like I am always told to do.

Still engrossed in the story of the princess, I run on to the Co-op and hand over the envelope to the lady. She opens it. 'This isn't money duck, it's a letter. You've brought me the wrong one.' I am ashamed; I have posted the milk check money. Now I really am in deep trouble.

My poor sister is distraught because she is looking after me and my dad, and he is being really difficult, so a silly little girl is not what she needs at all. She goes to see Mr Beer who runs the post office. Mr Beer is tall and thin, he is also very grumpy and I am afraid of him. But my big sister is not bothered at all – she faces him as I shelter behind her.

'Our Dulcie has posted the milk check money by mistake, silly little bugger,' Myrtle tells him.

'Nothing I can do, it's more than my job's worth to open the box now'.

He breathes in, pulls his lips together into a line, and pushes his thumbs into the pockets of his grey waistcoat. Mr Beer is a very grey man; he has grey hair, a grey suit and a grey face. His glasses have no rim and they sit somewhere on his nose. They argue for a while, Mr Beer getting very heated and pushing his fingers down hard into the pockets of his grey waistcoat. Myrtle stands her ground, becoming more insistent.

Then the postman comes to open the box and take away the letters. We are saved! Letter retrieved at last, Myrtle takes me by the hand down to the Co-op to collect the milk checks, lecturing me all the way there and back about how she'll tell our Mum what a nuisance I am and how she can't trust me to do anything.

63

Because I always lose my gloves, my mother has put them on a string so that they go through the sleeves of my coat. Somehow, I manage to lose my coat, and once more I am in trouble.

'I can't help it!' I wail as I am sent again to my bedroom. 'My head is full of things.'

'Full of cotton wool,' my mother says.

My parents' religion is the ogre of my childhood. It is there like a shadow, casting darkness onto everything. Dad is a Christadelphian because Mum wouldn't marry him unless he became one, so he is a reluctant believer. Every Sunday there is shouting because my Dad is taking too long to get ready to go to the Meeting. Shouts of 'Sam' get louder and more cross, and it always ends up with my mother walking with force into the entry, followed by my Dad running. I always hide underneath the big oak table on Sunday, pulling down the chenille cloth so I cannot be seen. I hate the shouting and the anger, so my first feelings are that I hate Christadelphians.

When I am older, I go to the Sunday school, which I quite like. Teddie Instone is our teacher. He has a kind red shiny face and I giggle, which makes him giggle too. In later years I am aware of my mother's disappointment because not one of us have followed her into the faith. Clive and Myrtle stopped going when they had finished Sunday school, just like I have. My Aunt Maud and Uncle Ralph have my cousin Doris, who is a Christadelphian, and I know that my mother would love us to be like her. Doris is nice, she is quiet and gentle, and she takes me to the Swanswell park with her. Doris is a special cousin, because my mum and her mum are sisters, and my dad and her dad are brothers.

Because my parents are Christadelphians, going to the pictures is wrong, swearing is wrong, and it seems to me that being happy or doing anything that brings pleasure is wrong. It is frowned upon to look into a mirror because that is vanity, which is a sin. We have an oval mirror hanging on the wall of the sitting room, so when I pass it, I take quick sidelong looks into it. I look at my chin and I don't like it, this is because I am vain, so I must stop looking or God will punish me. The fear of this God fills my young life, and follows me into my adult one. He is all seeing, and this is terrifying. I want proof of his existence, so I put a piece of cotton wool on my window ledge at night and ask God to prove he is there and make it wet. In the morning it is still dry, so I go triumphantly to my mother.

'See! God isn't listening; he hasn't answered my prayer.'

'God has more to do than listen to a silly little girl and her cotton wool,' I am told, but it doesn't satisfy me. The fear is still there but now there are doubts.

We do have a wireless and we are allowed to listen to that when my mother says so. The delights of the wireless are many; Children's Hour at five o'clock is a special time, when I sit down and listen to stories of Toy-town, and Larry the Lamb. As I get older I am allowed to listen to Dick Barton Special Agent at 6.45 each evening. Then there is Paul Temple, and later, H.G.Wells. 'War of the worlds' is broadcast each week, and we sit down to listen with a bowl of macaroni cheese. The wireless is a wonderful thing where I can listen to stories that feed my already fertile imagination. I can see each character in my mind. The magic of imagination without the instant gratification of pictures, because this is long before television arrives.

These are good times, settling down in the big chair and listening as stories unfold, doors opening into worlds beyond my own world. I can make them be anything I want them to be; places where people smile, no one shouts, and I am not invisible. Here I can be pretty, I can talk and I am not clumsy or stupid. There is music on the wireless too, but my mother switches it off when I want to hear it. The music is called Scherezade, and I am bewitched by its beauty. In its silencing, the threads to another world of magic are cut abruptly, and I am sad again. Life for me seems to be a mixture of restrictions and conflicting rules that create my unacceptable tantrums and frustrations. The confusion follows me into teenage and adult life, laying down patterns of belief which hold me tight, making me a prisoner of my past.

Chapter Ten

For the first five years of my life, my world is no bigger than a terraced house, a small garden, and a street. My brother and sister are much older than me, their presence in my world, vague and remote. Life is a pattern of wash-days, forty winks, bible readings and silence, and real life happens in my bedroom where I spend a lot of time. Here I have my special friends – imaginary friends with whom I share many things. There is Mary; she lives in a big house with me. We sit on the stairs and watch people come and go. They wear long dresses in silk, taffeta and satin, and the colours are rich greens the colour of emeralds, reds as deep as garnets. Around their necks are necklaces of deli-cate golden filigree and precious stones. Their hair hangs in heavy curls, moving as they dance like corn in a sum-mer field. We watch them from the imaginary stairs as they move to the lovely music, tossing their heads, smil-ing, whirling round and round. I tell Mary that I must be adopted because I know I am not wanted. My mother tells me often, 'I didn't want you', and it's nice to talk to Mary about it. As I lie in the uncomfortable dark at night, Mary is there to keep me away from the spiders, and if I watch the ladies dancing in their fine clothes for long enough, I will go to sleep.

It is the summer of 1942 when I go to Paradise Infants' school for the first time. The school is huge and strange as we line up in the hall, which has a high ceiling and is very dark. There are so many children, there is so much noise, and I am not sure where to go. Sitting in the centre, is a rocking horse. Such a thing none of us have ever seen before. We are children of the war, the back streets. Our dads are either away fighting or doing factory jobs like my Dad, who is a works policeman. There aren't many toys, our games mostly made from imagination, and a rocking horse is a strange sight. So, we stand in line, all hoping for a ride on this magnificent thing. Children are being lifted onto it, but somehow, I am not one of them. I hang back, get pushed to the back, and never get to sit on the rocking horse. I accept the disappointment as I accept everything, just because this is the way things are, and I am feeling overwhelmed by the strange surroundings.

Marylyn Wilkins, pretty bouncy curls and a big smile on her face, is being lifted onto the horse, and I watch her enviously. Her knickers fall down as we watch, but she shows no concern, just hoists them up and goes back to the line. I feel my face go pink; I am mortified on her behalf. If that had been me, I would have cried and found a place to hide in.

As I search around in the dark room of my memory, I find shadows, traces of people, their names, but mostly feelings in hidden corners: the first classroom, so alien to us all; the sitting still, the putting up of a hand if I want the lavatory, and the silence.

'Dulcie Matthews – go and stand in the corner.' It rings out now as clearly as then. I am talking when I should be silent – I am daydreaming when I should be listening.. Mostly, it is for talking, and not being able to answer questions because I haven't heard them, and sometimes for cheek. I am not sure what 'cheek' is. I have something to say, but when I say it, it is called cheek. This school business is going to be hard.

Gill Rowstron lives in Francis Street, and she calls for me. We walk to our school together. Her brother Bill knows my brother, so we are friends too. I go to Gill's house after school to play because her mother doesn't mind. The friendship we have made now is to stay with us, changing its form throughout our lives. As we get older, I spend long hours at Gill's house, her mother making me feel welcome at any time. Gill also has a piano, so I play 'The lost chord' or 'The holy city' and we both sing. Gill's little Scottish terrier Mac sits by my feet – puts back his head, and howls along with us. Going to the lavatory at Gills is scary, because it is at the very bottom of her garden. A wooden hut with the seat just a plank of wood and a hole, that's all there is, and we go together, giggling, whispering our secrets.

At eight years old I move to Edgewick junior school; We walk along Cross Road in little groups, no hurry to arrive, anxious to extend our playing time. We pick leaves from an over-hanging laurel bush to put in our shoes. If they go brown it means that someone we love also loves us. This doesn't impress the owner of the laurel bush, and we run quickly away, his shouts following us up the street.

Winter has come, and the playground is covered with snow, trodden down to a hard crust. We make slides across it, running, then leaning forward, as we trust our feet to the mirror surface spanning the playground concrete. I am afraid of this feeling of losing control, not wanting to fall and lose face – I take a deep breath and go for it, relaxing into the glorious feeling of freedom as my feet take me with them. We wait for playtime so that we can have our bottle of milk and throw snowballs. On the way home from school we make more slides on the pavements, but salt is sprinkled on them and they melt.

I stand in the outside lavatory and listen as boys climb the wall and ask to see our knickers. Some girls lift up their skirts to show navy bloomers. They giggle and run back into the classroom.

I want to make a friend, so I ask Iris who lives in Nuffield Road if she will come to tea. After school, we go together to her house, and I wait while her mother puts her in a pretty dress and curls her hair with iron tongs that she heats on the fire first. Iris's hair sizzles when the tongs are wound into it. We walk back to my house, but the gate is locked. My mother comes to the gate and I ask her, 'Iris has come to play, can she stay for tea?'

My mother looks surprised and then indignant. Her head goes up and her mouth goes into a tight bunch. 'Of course not, go and play,' she says, so, I walk back with Iris to explain to her mother. Her mother is very angry with me, she calls me a little liar, and I walk home again crying. I sit on the kerb, my feet in the gutter and I stay like that for a long time before wandering away to the entry behind Flo's house. Pink willow herb grows out of the broken walls, bending out and upwards towards the light. I pick some to take in for my mother; maybe she will have my tea ready for me now. Flo lives with Joe; she has a bony wrinkled face with lots of make-up on it. The lipstick leaks into small lines around her mouth, and she smells of perfume. Joe is very small, bald and bent, and people talk about them. I wonder about them too, trying to understand what I hear.

In fact, I am finding it increasingly difficult to hear. I sit at the back of the classroom and watch as Miss Humphries writes with scratchy chalk on the blackboard, but I can't hear what she says. Now she rubs the writing off again with the felt rubber, and a dusty cloud of chalk rises into the classroom. The smell gets into my nostrils and makes me cough. I am talking, so the board rubber is thrown in my direction. I am afraid of Miss Humphries; she has a screwed up face, her mouth and eyes seem to disappear into lines, and she is always angry. She calls me to the front. 'Dulcie Matthews, you are not listening again!'

'I *am*,' I answer, 'but I can't hear you!'

I am sent to see Mr Wills, and I stand in his room looking at my feet. Mr Wills, white hair, stooping shoulders, and glasses that move about as he talks, is a kind headmaster who seems a little bit afraid of Miss Humphries too. I am told that because I don't listen, I can't sing in the hall with the others. I am stopped from joining in the dancing too, and I feel angry.

'Shut your mouth girl!' It's Miss Humphries again. 'Just because you are gormless, you don't have to look gormless.'

But my mouth won't shut. I am breathing through it because I can't breathe through my nose. My sister is now married and lives in Canal Road, so I run to my sister after school. Myrtle is angry on my behalf, she goes to the school while I trail behind her struggling to keep up, to see Mr Wills, and fights my battles for me.

They have found out that I cannot hear because my tonsils and adenoids need to come out. At home I am now called adenoid Annie because I can't breathe through my nose at all, and I have to go into hospital.

The hospital is even more frightening than sirens and air-raid shelters. There are lots of us, all waiting for our operation, and no one explains anything. We lie side by side in hard metal beds whispering to each other until we are wheeled into the corridor. Here, we are left in a line, and I am at the end. The children who have had their operation are wheeled past us, one at a time, their white gowns covered in blood. My life seems to be a sequence of lines in which I await something dreadful.

By the time I get into the theatre I am hysterical. They hold me down, cover my face with cotton wool, then there is a bright light that comes closer and closer to my face, pressing me down onto the table. I can smell something awful and I can't stand it any more, so I struggle. Then it is all over and I wake up feeling sick in the ward again, my arms covered in scratches. The Irish girl in the bed next to me cries all night asking for water. We cannot talk, my throat hurts really badly and still, no one has explained what is happening, but I do know that something has been taken away from my throat, and I am afraid that I will never be able to talk again.

At home again I am kept in bed while they all joke that 'our kid has had her voice removed', but it does have compensations. My sister is now in the ATS. She comes home on leave to see me, running into my bedroom in her khaki uniform with her little hat balanced on the side of her head. Black shining curls burst out from beneath it. She smells of fresh air and roses, and her cheeks are cold.

'Maybelle, look what I've bought you – do you like her?'

In her hands is a little black doll, and I reach out to hold it. 'Her name is Topsy,' I say.

My brother's girlfriend comes too, bringing me a red

bangle engraved with roses and leaves. This is wonderful! My mother keeps coming up with warm soothing drinks and soup, and life has never been so good. Being ill, it seems, brings about the harmony and attention I need so much.

I am now in the top class that is ruled by Miss Courts. She is small and fat with a pink face and fluffy white hair and wears glasses without any rim. Her eyes are fierce behind them. She sits me at the front because my reputation has preceded me and I am known to chatter, but this doesn't help me to avoid trouble. Someone at the back of the class has started to draw a little picture. It is then folded and passed on to the next one, who adds their bit, folds it and passes it on again. I am at the front, so it reaches me last of all. I add my bit to the picture, which, when opened out, is rude. Miss Courts sees me with the scrap of paper and calls me out to the front. She looks at the picture, looks around the class, and I am shamed.

'Dulcie is a disgraceful little girl and no-one must speak to her,' the class is told. So my wooden desk is pulled right out to the front of the class and there I sit – in silence. I feel dirty and ashamed, also angry because everyone has contributed, and I am being punished. This latest happening takes my sister back to see Mr Wills. I am reinstated in the classroom, but the stigma will not go away.

We have a new girl in our class. She is from Russia and her name is Luba Rozlomek. Luba has blond plaits and cannot speak very good English, so we are all kind to her. It has something to do with the war, which has only been over for two years. We are all fascinated by Luba. In our young lives there has never been anyone foreign, so this is a new experience. We all want to play with her and everyone is nice. We also have another teacher come to us. He is called Mr Huxter and I like him a lot. He has this trick with his ears, so that if we chatter or misbehave, instead of shouting, he wiggles his ears. It works like magic, we become compliant instantly.

Underwear is now a big problem for me, as we have to strip down to our pants for games in the hall and I am so ashamed of my liberty bodice and knickers. The liberty bodice is made of cream fleecy material with rubber buttons, and it grips my chest tightly. My knickers are made by my mother from Courtaulds wincyette, which is itchy on the inside. They almost cover my thighs and pull right up above my waist. I find that it is easier to survive the embarrassment if I turn it into a joke, so I make a big deal of scratching. It makes the other children laugh, and my face is saved.

Joy Taylor is in my class; she is a dainty, pretty girl with beautiful underslips and knickers made by her mother. The slips are silky and have a circle of lace on them and a 'J' embroidered in the centre. How I long for pretty underwear like hers – I tell my mother but she doesn't understand. So, I continue to wear my itchy bloomers and to be the class clown. We all learn to survive in the best ways we can. Life is a series of survivals, and habits form when we are children that remain with us. Sometimes they serve our purpose, often times they hinder our progress. This is how life is...

Children are having birthday parties, and I want to have one too. My mother says no, and I am too wise to argue. Myrtle lives with Len and her little girl Stephanie, so I go to tell her.

'I'll do you a party, Maybelle,' she tells me – and she does. The only party I ever have, and it is my sister who gives it for me. For a long time before, I write lists of names. I haven't any notebooks, so I write in my special 'Wonder Book of Fairy Stories' given to me by Len. They are still there, those names on my list. Michael Baker is written there, not once, but four times.

The fantasy life of my mind spills over into reality when I play with Julie and Geoffrey Lowe after school. They live in Edgewick Road, so I go home with them.

'She says she's the Fairy Queen,' Julie taunts, echoed by Geoffrey.

'Fairy Queen, Fairy Queen!' he chants as they laugh. I really believe I am the Fairy Queen, but they hit me, punch me in my face, so I run home to sit on the pavement and watch the sun making long shadows as it drops out of sight behind the houses. I can't be the fairy queen after all, and the harsh reality of being just me is almost too much to bear.

Where can I escape to now? Playing 'out' after school helps; we run down to the 'cut' where a thick rope has been tied to an over-hanging branch. The braver among us grip the rope, wrapping our legs round it and swinging out over the canal. Eventually tiring of the thrill, we wander back to the street to play hopscotch or leapfrog. Swinging over the rail by the bus-stop can also pass time, but I am never very good at this, often falling and banging my head – so I watch instead.

Lots of us are scratching our heads, so we queue up to see the nit nurse. My hair is very long and thick, and I have nits! I am so ashamed; I go to the chemist and wait outside for the shop to open. Looking around to see whether anyone is listening, I whisper, 'Can I have some durbar soap please'.

'Speak up duck!'

I try again a bit louder, hand my money over the counter, grab the soap and run home. Then comes the washing and the rubbing. The soap smells horrible and I complain, my voice muffled by the large rough towel, my head between my dad's knees. My mother sits me at the kitchen table and goes to work with the nit comb. I become fascinated by the tiny black things she is combing out and cracking with her nails. The association of lice crawling in my hair isn't made with these strange things on the table.

At school the following day, we compare notes, all shame now gone in our shared experience.

Chapter Eleven

We have taken our 11-plus exams and forgotten about them. It is the summer holidays and we are free from the confines of classroom and order for this wonderful long time. We can run in the street, around the entrys and over the common – we can play on the rope that swings out over the canal or just wander about talking. Sitting on the front step, I have a wooden bobbin from my mother's workbox with four nails in the top. A ball of wool in my pocket, I do french knitting, making long chains which I will then stitch into mats. The cardboard tops from milk bottles are also useful. These I poke the hole out from the centre and wind wool round and round. They make big fat pom-poms, and the pleasure of making them lasts all through the summer.

Roller skates are the thing of the moment; I have some too, but my balance is dreadful, so I spend more time on my bottom or watching everyone else. I wear just one, strapping the heavy skate to my right foot and scooting about that way.

The results arrive from our 11-plus exam, and I have passed, so I get the promised bike, my very first one. I wonder how I managed to pass as I didn't try and didn't really feel that it was important. School is just the place I go to from under my mother's feet. My Aunt Lou is really pleased; they have never rated me very highly, my mother's two sisters. They like Myrtle and Clive and I am just an afterthought who gets in everyone's way and day-dreams.

So now I have achieved something at last, and Aunt Lou buys me a brown leather satchel that smells of horses, and a tennis racket in its wooden press. My uniform is bought, off the peg, and because I still can't ride my bike, I walk over the common to Stoke Park Grammar school. This is somewhere I have never been, and I greet this extension to my world with eager anticipation.

The big day has arrived. Feeling uncomfortable and strange in my navy uniform and stiff white blouse, I put the new shiny satchel on my back with its ruler and pencils inside, and I walk over the common, along Swan Lane and into Dane Road where my new, very big school is waiting. We are filed into a classroom where we sit down at desks, which are bigger than the ones at Edgewick School, and we are introduced to our form mistress. We are all nervous as we try to find out each other's names and to make friends for ourselves. Some girls are quiet, some bold and I don't know anyone. Gill Rowstron has been sent to another form, but I quickly learn new names and faces.

We are given a timetable and told which classroom we have to find, which is so very frightening. Long corridors with a staircase at each end and so many rooms. There are only girls here, and as the bell rings for the end of lessons, the corridors teem with girls, rushing in different directions to find their next classroom. I get lost often in the first weeks, getting constant scolding for being late. There is a different teacher for each lesson, and a pattern of behaviour quickly sets itself, as I once again become the clown, behaving badly. Homework is set each day, but I never do it. Some days I am withdrawn and sad in class because there has been yet another row with my mother in the morning. These rows always end with me getting angry and shouting, 'I don't care!' and my mother saying I am wicked and that she can never forgive me for my wilful behaviour. I flounce out of the gate, then forget it all until home time comes around.

Then, I dawdle on the way home over the common, delaying the inevitable moment of going through the gate because I know that now, my mother will refuse to speak to me for weeks, unless I say sorry. These times are often, and usually end with me pushing a note under her bedroom door with my written apology, just so that she will speak to me again. The silent times are painful for me, hurting me inside, so that an apology is the only solution. I feel lonely, isolated – a barrier of silence separating me from what is happening around me. It is as though all the voices are coming from a long way away. To be ignored, this is the worst punishment of all. It makes me invisible again, and it also makes me very angry.

We arrive at school each morning, rushing through corridors, dashing into classrooms and getting books together. Then I ask someone, 'Have you done your English homework?' Mostly the answer is 'yes', so I hurriedly copy something into my book before handing it in. Doing homework doesn't seem a priority to me as my parents don't seem to even know it exists. There is a total lack of interest in my daytime activities at home.

Games, I decide, are a waste of time. I hate the conformity of it all, so I soon develop my own way of making it more bearable. Hockey sticks are great for tripping people up, until I am sent off for bad behaviour. Tennis too, has its moments; I am left-handed, so if I do my practice shots standing on the right of a right-hander, I can cause mayhem in very little time. Netball is another penance to be endured.

As with gym, a shower always follows these happenings, which is the biggest nightmare of all. At twelve, my body is changing, and the liberty bodices are now very uncomfortable. Other girls are appearing in pretty white lace bras, and my mother steadfastly refuses to get me one. 'You're not old enough,' she insists, until Myrtle finally intervenes and she gives in. But oh dear! When it arrives, it is peach satin with cups encased in circles and circles of stitching.

'I look like an amazon warrior!' I wail. 'I *can't* wear this!' Now I am ungrateful, I am never satisfied, so I wear it and endure the teasing of my classmates, trying whenever possible to avoid the shower room and its humiliation.

The gym lesson is dreaded because I just cannot gambol like the other girls. I leap over the vaulting horse, then run quickly over the mat, hoping not to be seen. No matter how I try, the fear of falling forwards is greater than the teasing or the trouble I am in for avoiding the somersault.

We are changing quickly, our bodies are doing strange things – we move between laughter and unexplained misery. Whispers in the lavatories about periods are greeted with a mixture of longing and fear. I have no idea what periods are, but in some way I know that I will be more grown up if I have them. A few girls have already joined this elite group of the initiated; they huddle together in corners of the classroom to compare, and I feel excluded. They have moved on to a new stage of existence and we, the uninitiated, are still children, not to be included in the furtive conversations in corners.

Then it is my turn, but the life-changing event is not greeted with the enthusiasm I had anticipated. I am in my bedroom when I notice the dark stain on my navy knickers, and I am embarrassed. I go down to the sitting room where my sister is sitting, and show her, my face scarlet. Myrtle laughs and calls my mother in from the kitchen. 'Our kid has started her periods.' Mum comes in and between them they produce a narrow pink elastic belt with two hooks on it. My mother gives me an oblong pad of sheet that she has machined together and they show me how to wear it. I am mortified; I run from the room to the safety of my bedroom, where I cry into my pillow until Myrtle comes in and says gently, 'It's alright, our kid, it happens to all of us.'

The business of periods is not glamorous at all, and the monthly chore of soaking the machined pads in cold water and them boiling them in an old bucket on the gas stove is a hated job. Trying not to let my Dad see them is difficult too. Wearing them is another cross to be borne, as they chafe the inside of my legs and make changing in the shower room even more difficult than liberty bodices and Boudicca bras.

The school grounds are my joy and delight; lots of open field and tarmac paths to wander along during break. Trees border the playing field, so I can watch new buds followed by leaves, then the Autumn pleasure of catching the crispy brown leaves as they float downwards. If we catch one we can make a wish, so each break time we rush off to the trees making our wishes as we run. We sit on the steps playing five stones. This is the favourite game of the moment, and we all seem to have a pocket containing five little ridged squares, prepared to play if anyone is willing.

Lessons become times for me to daydream. The classroom looks out towards a churchyard, and as I look towards it, the teacher's voice becomes a drone with no shape, just sound. I write poems about death and trees in the back of my exercise books. My dreams are fractured suddenly with 'Dulcie, what did I just say?' I cannot answer, so end up getting order marks for inattention. The offending material written without permission in my exercise books is torn out, ripped up and thrown away. I am made to pay for another book, and no one even bothered to read what I had written! The injustice makes me angry; I am often angry now, with so many things: my mother, restrictions that expect me to conform, rules which I hate, and the posh kids. Before I arrive at this school, my friends are all from around Silverton Road, but these girls speak in a different way from me, and I rebel against the difference.

We now have a form teacher called Mrs Bunney. She doesn't approve of the scholarship children, feeling that we lower the tone and standard of the Grammar School. In our leisure time we are now going to the local dance at the 'Matrix', and we know that Mrs Bunney's brother is the bandleader. This gives us an edge; we can use this to level up the score. So, when Mrs Bunney, feeling particularly irate, calls us Guttersnipes, I am so very angry that I stand up, grip my desk with my fingers, and shout 'We *are not* guttersnipes!'

An awful silence follows my outburst; Mrs Bunney stands back, draws a deep breath and says, 'Go to Miss Nixon's office immediately!'

I walk out, head in the air, anger showing in every step, to wait outside the Head Mistress's room. Everyone is convinced that I will be expelled; no-one has dared before to challenge Mrs Bunney, so when I face Miss Nixon, small and mild in her manner, I am defiant in my refusal to apologise.

I tell Miss Nixon what Mrs Bunney has called us scholarship children, and wait for the verdict. Mrs Bunney is called into the room, and I stand silently, wondering what is going to happen next, and how I will tell my mother what I have done. There will be a lecture about how much I am like my dad, and how he defied authority in the army and was sent to the glass house. Or how he got the sack from Courtaulds before he lost his arm, because he punched his boss. 'You and your Dad, you just won't accept authority,' I can hear her telling me.

Now Miss Nixon is actually reprimanding Mrs Bunney – in front of me! She is told that she must apologise to me for the offensive remark. I return to the classroom feeling vindicated, vowing to toe the line now that I have known justice.

Sadly, my behaviour doesn't improve as I move through the school. Maths I find particularly hard, so these lessons become a stage on which to play. My ruler and pencils are tossed out of the window, and there I am, my friend Ronnie holding my legs while I grovel about on the tarmac through the open window, trying to retrieve them. We go to our Physics lesson, which I also find hard, and with my friends, I turn my stool over, cover it with my green science overall and crawl about at the back of the classroom. I turn the taps upward to spray water on the ceiling; my behaviour is particularly subversive.

We have Art lessons in the upstairs room, so someone makes an excuse to go to the lavatory, passing the tray of sticky buns, which sit under the stairs waiting for breaktime. One or two buns find their way into a gymslip pocket, the illicit bounty shared and eaten later. What promotes this way of behaving, I am not sure. Is it the classic rebellion of a working-class girl, or a reaction to a stern and severe parent? Or am I naturally a discipline-hating clown who is wilful and disobedient? Or maybe this is just boundary testing in the process of growing up.

My English literature lesson is here, and I want to listen to the poems. Miss Findlay is reading us a poem by Harold Monroe, it is called 'Overheard on a salt marsh' and it is all about a goblin that wants the green glass beads. I am enchanted by the words; I want more and more. We read 'Kubla Khan' and I am walking in caves 'measureless to man'. I listen to every word; I write essays and get top marks. This is something I understand, I feel and taste the words, the rhythm of each line carries me along.

Our music lessons are my other joy, and I run to the classroom, arriving first. Miss Marchant is playing us some music by Debussy today. This is a new world, only briefly glimpsed before to be snatched away from me. She is playing 'a l'apres-midi d'un faune', explaining to us that this is a tone poem and Debussy is painting a picture of a hot lazy afternoon, and a fawn wandering amongst the trees, slowly. How wonderful is this music; no distraction from girls who are not interested and vie for my attention will take my mind away from this magic. It ends, and Miss Marchant says, 'Well girls, what did you think of it?'

'It's beautiful, beautiful,' I say.

She points her ruler at me. 'Is that *all* you can say Dulcie Matthews?' she says, and I burst into tears. She has spoiled the magic. She finds me as odd as my mother finds me. I feel silly, and somehow dirty, soiled.

Miss Marchant is contrite. 'I'm sorry, Dulcie,' she tells me, and I understand that she is not feeling good today, but the hurt doesn't go away – it doesn't go away at all.

Music is infinitely more interesting to me than playing hockey, which seems such a silly thing to do. Everyone gets excited and runs about shouting, and I do not see the point. So getting sent off for foul play again is advantageous. I make my way to the music room where I know there is a piano. If I am careful, I won't be found.

I sit down and begin to play the tunes I know by ear. My lessons with Mr Coleman finished long ago when I passed my Grade I, but I have never stopped playing, and trying to read music. I am engrossed in the piano, so the door opening suddenly makes me jump. Miss Cooke, our music teacher, is standing in the doorway looking at me. I like Miss Cooke, though she is very stern; she is also kind, never cruel with words. There is intensity in her stare, the severity accentuated by yellow-grey hair pulled back into a bun, with wisps around her face which have escaped, as if doing her hair is just an afterthought, a necessity to be dispensed with quickly. Her face is yellow, tired and lined. She says, 'Carry on, Dulcie', and she listens! No one ever listens to me so I am nervous, but somehow she seems to know that I can do it.

'Should you be in here?' she asks me.

Here it comes, I think. 'No Miss Cooke, I've been sent off the playing field.'

'In that case, you must have a detention, but I would like to give you some piano lessons,' she tells me.

'My mum can't afford lessons, Miss Cooke,' I tell her.

But she says that she doesn't want any money, so I have the lessons, and I really practise because she believes in me and says I am musical and gifted. I have never been told this before, and I work so hard. Before Miss Cooke leaves the school I have reached Grade V, and she gives me a big bundle of piano music when she leaves.

Miss Cooke plays the piano for us all to file into prayers in the morning. 'Ronda a la Turka' rings out and we all march in time to the music.

Hazel Williams is in the next class to me, and her auburn ringlets are the envy of the school. As she walks into the hall, they bounce, springing up and down in time. I ask my mother if I can have ringlets, and she really does try. She puts rags into my hair at night, but my strong thick hair just will not do as it is told, and by dinnertime the curls have gone again.

I have been asked to read the prayer in the Hall this morning, which is an honour. I am not sure why I have been singled out but it feels important, so I must do my best. I stand behind the stage waiting to climb up in front of the school, my heart is thumping and I am trembling. My moment comes and I mount the stage, read my piece slowly and clearly, then return to my line. There is laughter, because I have one sock up, and the other one is down round my ankles. I am unwittingly the clown again, even when I want to be taken seriously.

Chapter Twelve

Memory can play tricks, leaving some things clearly imprinted, while the reasons for them become elusive. I now have a teacher called Mr Hurst, who comes to the house and gives me piano lessons at half price. He comes from the Coventry School of Music, so I am honoured – and yet I cannot recall the reason for this honour. He sends me across the city to Earlsdon. I am to play for a man with the possibility of joining the Youth Orchestra when I am a few years older.

Earlsdon is posh, and I have never been here before. I am shown into a room that takes both my breath and my tongue away. This room is nothing like our tiny dark room at home. It is so big and so light. The window goes down to the floor, and through it I can see trees and lawns. The carpet is a deep glowing red, my feet almost disappearing into the pile. Then I see the piano; a grand piano, white and shining is by the window. I stop, and look in amazement and wonder. A man's voice is saying, 'Well, come on then, what are you going to play for me?'

'I can't play *that*!'

He looks at me, puzzled by my reaction. I have never seen such a beautiful piano, and I am afraid to touch it. Then, somehow, I manage to begin, the keys feeling like silk beneath my fingers.

'You have promise,' he tells me. 'Practise, and I'll hear you again in a year.'

But I don't practise, and so the first of my opportunities slides away from me. I lack the dedication needed, and, as is so often the way with gifts, I take my gift for granted. It would be easy to blame lack of interest on the part of my parents, but other people have succeeded in the same circumstances. I must accept my own lack of persistence.

Boys have become a distraction, something to talk about in excited groups at break time. Kathleen Wilson , worldly and experienced, answers my questions. She has already had a boyfriend, and tells me that boys like to touch you *'there'*. She points to her bust and smiles a knowing smile. This doesn't sound nice at all.

The chain link fence bordering the playing field is now leaned on during break, as girls talk to boys, pressing their faces against the wire, touching fingers and kissing. Some girls seem to have lots of boys hovering for them, but with a few others, I hang back and watch. This new interest in boys needs thinking about. I am still at the stage of crushes. Some of us have a crush on the head girl; in our innocence we follow her around the school, opening doors and carrying books. We still live in an innocent age where talk of homosexuality is non-existent and unknown, so we have no hang-ups about our sexuality, we are just developing in a normal way, exploring our feelings.

Blushing is my nightmare, my face colouring into a deep glowing pink at every tiny embarrassment, imagined or real. I hide behind a curtain of hair – I hang down my head, waiting for the flush to pass.

I now go to the Methodist church on the corner of Cross Road, and also to the youth club on the corner of Broad Street. Dave Keogh goes there too, and I like him a lot. Tall, with a slow smile and gentle manner, he makes me feel safe. He rides his bike slowly by my side as I walk home. He lives in Stoke, and I see him as I cycle home from school. Older than me, he is a police cadet. I loiter now on the way home, hoping to see him.

In the summer holidays I go to play with Margaret Mason who lives in Old Church Road. A boy named Tommy lives by her, and I spend a lot of time watching him from Margaret's bedroom window. He loiters on the pavement, calling up to me. Long hot sunny summer days, with me in a banana-coloured cotton frock, my long hair hanging loose as I lean out of the window. He waits for me every day, but I soon tire, and move on to some new distraction.

These first new stirrings are exquisite and frightening. Beautiful in their innocence, they remain unsullied in my memory.

My very first kiss is at the Methodist Hall Social. I am dancing with Brian Coleman who lives over the road, and we stand, awkward, reach across the space between us, and tentatively kiss. Our noses get in the way, we move back, embarrassed and each secretly disappointed by the encounter.

I am in the school choir with my friend Veronica Radburn, and Speech Day is looming. It is to be in the Central Hall and the Mayor will be there. We are in the front row in full view of the Mayor, Miss Nixon and all the dignitaries, wearing our school blazers and looking very smart. We sing 'Jerusalem' with gusto, and then stand up to sing the first song. Ronnie nudges me, I look at her, she chops her arm with one hand and slowly appears to be pulling her arm out of her blazer sleeve. I giggle, she giggles, the giggles get more urgent and we can't stop. Tears are now falling down our faces and we are uncontrollable.

Speech Day ends, and we are sent for in Miss Nixon's study. We are reprimanded, and stand with our heads down looking at our feet. No giggling now, this is serious. We are thrown out of the choir and barred from ever singing in it again. Luckily I don't have the problem of telling my mother because she is disinterested and didn't go to the Speech Day anyway.

School reports become the topic of conversation at the end of each term. Examination results are read out loud to the class, starting from the bottom. There is a ripple of subdued laughter when our Maths results are read: 'Dulcie Matthews – two', followed by the usual lecture about playing around and not listening.

'Dulcie is always top in Maths if I start at the bottom.' Miss Marshall's words cause me no problem – I hate Maths and have no understanding of it, so I am not worried. I carefully open my report on the way home, then stick it back, ready to hand over. My mother looks at it, shrugs, and puts it onto the table. I read 'Dulcie is insubordinate', but have no idea what that means. I ask my mother, who gives me the dictionary, and I never forget its meaning again. 'Dulcie is a clever girl who just talks too much and doesn't take lessons seriously.' 'Dulcie is extremely musical and could do so much better.' 'Dulcie excels at English language and literature, but is too ready to be distracted.' Each year the comments remain the same, but I am not reprimanded, and the subject of my school behaviour is never discussed.

Uniform is a bone of contention throughout my school life. I hate wearing it because it makes me look like everyone else, and I don't want to do what I am told. As soon as I am out of the school grounds, off comes my red beret, to be crammed into a pocket. Socks roll down to my ankles, sleeves pushed up and blazer tied round my waist. This morning I am asked to go to the staff room to see Miss Smallwood. She is a tiny lady with soft white hair and glasses, wearing always a tweed skirt and jacket. She teaches us Scripture and we affectionately call her Isaiah because her eyes have a habit of shooting above her glasses and one does seem higher than the other. She has seen me outside school and reprimands me on my appearance. I prepare for defiance, sticking out my lips, but she says, 'Dulcie, you look so nice in your uniform, it's a shame not to wear it properly.' What a clever lady! I wear my beret from this day forward, proving that flattery will get you anywhere at all.

Cookery classes are weekly, and we arrive with our domestic aprons, our ingredients in a bag. Today we make shortbreads, which are packed into my satchel to carry home. Going home needs to be delayed again today because my mother is not speaking to me, so Ronnie walks home with me. We push my bike between us, and stop over the common to lean on the bridge. Now, we take out the still warm shortbread and eat it. I watch Ronnie's feet; they are slim and brown inside her dark green court shoes. I remember Ronnie's lovely feet, even when we are both old. They fascinate me, all the tiny bones moving as she walks. She walks all the way home with me, an ally against my mother, then turns around to walk all the way back, leaving me to face the silence of my homecoming.

We are approaching our last year, and walking round the tarmac paths discussing boys, dancing and what we are going to do. I love to hear the sound of my shoes on the tarmac path; it is comforting. We wear ward shoes – our indoor shoes inside school, but I sneak outside in mine because of the sound they make. Each new pair of shoes

I have had throughout my life has been tested by walking up the garden path; it is the last thing I do as a woman before my home goes forever from me. If they squeak, my mother says, 'That's because I haven't paid for them', but I know she is joking, as my mother is strict about money.

'Never owe anyone anything,' she tells me. When she goes to bed, her carefully saved money in its' box is taken upstairs with her to keep it safe.

I excel at Music, English and Domestic Science. Our Form Mistress has suggested to me that I might consider university. I would just need to get a good grade in Maths or Science as well. I run home to tell my mother, but I am told 'Working class girls don't go to university, we have got you a nice job at Courtaulds in the office.' This is it; I accept the verdict, forget it and carry on with my life, but I lose interest in school completely.

Crossing the divide between where I live and where lots of my classmates live is a difficult journey. This other world is genteel and very appealing. I am invited to tea at Barbara Fessey's house. She lives in a big house in Dane road, near to our school. The day is sunny, and we sit in her garden beneath big trees, while her mother, who is very slim and pretty, brings out tea on a tray. This is how I would like to live, and I feel very comfortable. Her mother smiles a lot and is very nice to me and to Barbara.

Adjusting to the realisation of another world beyond Silverton Road is not easy. Suddenly, girls have 'Mummies and Daddies', not 'Mums and Dads' like mine. They come to school in cars, and their uniforms are beautifully tailored. The uniform, chosen to close the gap between classes, becomes just another barrier, as I compare my ill-fitting 'off-the-peg' tunic with theirs.

Thursday is my favourite day. On Thursday I go home with Ronnie at lunchtime, where her mother cooks me liver and onions. Ronnie has three sisters and her home is happily busy. Onions frying in the pan smell wonderful, and the easy banter between Ronnie's mother and sisters feels comfortable. I want so much to have a home like this, with a welcoming mother and sisters to talk to. My sister is twelve years older than I am, and my brother is ten years older. I am a lonely, solitary child, isolated from companionship and by my mother's stern silences. Other people's homes and families are my substitute, my place of refuge before I go back home to the silence, the order and the Bible readings.

Chapter Thirteen

It is the Christmas holiday, I am fifteen years old and desperately need to supplement my income. I go dancing and want pretty dresses. On the Foleshill Road there is a dress shop run by the Misses Payne, and in the window there is a lilac blue taffeta dress. It has a big circular skirt, and I dream about wearing it to Selbourne Hall where I go to dancing classes with Beryl and Jean Parker. My classes are paid for by Phil, who is a lot older than I am. He wants me to be his dancing partner and to take bronze, silver and gold medals with him, so he pays for me.

Dancing is now my joy and obsession. In my silver shoes and full skirts I become that other person, the one who lives inside me. I move to the music becoming oblivious to anything else. The classes are taken by Alf and Hettie. Alf, a small dapper man with a big moustache, has danced with Hettie in many competitions and they are very good. Hettie is slender with bright blonde hair swept back from her face into a roll. Her skin is almost white, her lips, a crimson shiny contrast. We dance to the music of Victor Sylvester on a gramophone which sometimes sticks, making the music play over and over again.

I need to buy the dress, so I sign on to do the Christmas post. Loaded up with a heavy sack, I set out optimistically on my round. This is a cold winter, the snow has started to thaw, then frozen again into hard dangerous ridges on the pavements. I still have an almost full sack because so many of the addresses are to houses that are no longer standing. The gaps where they should be are now just rubble, a crumbling reminder of a war not long over. A kind gentleman in Station Street takes pity on me because I drop the letters on his step. He takes me in and his wife makes me a mug of hot tea. I wrap my hands around the mug, feeling the blood slowly creep back into my fingers.

Off I go again, but it is getting dark and I need to go to the toilet so badly it hurts. Too shy to ask someone, I cannot hold it any longer. The warm liquid runs slowly down my legs and into my new boots. I limp home, each step agony as I squelch through the frozen snow. My mum and dad are wonderful! They dry me out, find me warm socks and more shoes, then we all set off together to deliver the long overdue mail. Never again! I buy the dress, but I am not convinced that it was worth the trouble.

The Misses Payne become an important part of my weekends. Their shop is very ramshackle and old fashioned. I sit in the back room having 'a cuppa' with Miss Edith Payne amongst numerous boxes and pieces of tissue paper. The boxes are scattered around the room, piled on top of each other. There never seems to be any space, but I love these Saturday mornings. Miss Payne is very tall; her hair is grey and frizzy, pulled into an untidy bun and held at the side with brown sidecombs. One eye is slightly off focus, and I find this very disconcerting, as I am never sure whether she is looking at me or not. She has bunions, so her enormous feet have holes cut into the leather to allow her bunions room. She is kind, and she listens to me, so I confide in her. Sometimes, when a really nice dress comes in, I try it on, and she puts it onto one side. I take some money in every week until I can pay for it.

Edith Paynes' sister rarely comes to the shop. When she does, she is brisk and slightly disapproving. I think the vague faded atmosphere of dusty elegance, and the chaos surrounding her sister are too much for her. She is very different from Edith, having a love of order.

The summer of July 1953 has arrived, and I am free from school! We go into town and have our photographs taken; the euphoria of release feeling wonderful. I am going on holiday to a camp in North Wales with Beryl and Jean Parker. I am sixteen and they are a few years older, so my parents are happy about me going.

Arriving at the camp, we pitch our tent and go to fill our sleeping bags with straw. The discomfort doesn't matter, it is all too new and different. In the morning we fry bread in a pan over a gas ring, smother it in brown sauce, and nothing has ever tasted so good. There are dark good-looking Welsh boys there, so the euphoric freedom is delicious. Our liaisons are conducted with smiles, touched hands, and the idle yet so important conversations of innocence, unsullied by the pressures of carnal knowledge.

On my return home, it is now time for me to go to work. My mother and father have arranged for me to work in an office at Courtaulds, so the next stage in the life of a 'back street kid' is about to begin…

Chapter Fourteen

My Dad is a man among men; not a tall man, but slightly built and quick moving. His bony face is lined and tanned from hours spent on his allotment. He has the strong Matthews chin that juts out defiantly when he feels cornered. He is bent forward, not in a defeated way, but with an urgency of movement, as if the very act of leaning will help him get there even faster. His one remaining hand rubs his face and his knee in short nervous strokes, especially when engrossed in his beloved Westerns. Blue-grey eyes are always looking beyond me to a space somewhere over my shoulder. He has a vague, disappointed expression, at times slightly wondering, maybe at the mystery of what has turned out as his life. A gentle man with sense of humour amazingly still in tact, he carefully avoids strife by disappearing expertly into the greenhouse, or to the allotment, so that his presence just seems to fade. Yet in the big things of life, he is there, facing up to them with the quiet courage which is his trademark, and ultimately it is my mother who is the great avoider.

How do I separate the threads of his being from the fabric that is my life? His constant background presence and my total belief in his love for me have helped to weave a backcloth which has sustained me through so many crises. Although he died in 1982, he is still just a thought away from reality.

Despite the avoidance and gentleness, in defence of his youngest daughter he could be fierce. Mr Wilkins, the old man next door, shouts at me because I am bouncing my ball against his wall, or playing hopscotch on the pavement outside his door, and there is my Dad, facing up to Mr Wilkins in my defence. The stump, which is all there is left of his right arm, quivers with rage and indignation. He lost his right arm before I was born, to a machine belt at Courtaulds factory. He was caught up in the belt and taken round with it, his arm sliced off like a rasher of bacon. Afterwards, he picked it up and, refusing all help, walked unassisted to the ambulance. Years later, my brother worked with the fireman who had driven the ambulance.

'Stubborn old bugger – wouldn't go on the stretcher,' is my brother's comment when relating the story to me. He says it with the pride we both feel for this man among men. Years later still, in the tiny north Lancashire village of Warton, I was to meet a man who had also witnessed my father's bravery, and find myself wishing that he was here now, so that I could tell him all the things so taken for granted during his lifetime. He never did great things, or made great waves in the world, but he faced it with dignity and forbearance – leaving lasting pleasure in his memories.

At six years old, the world is a loud and uncertain place, and my bedroom is a dark, threatening abyss. My nights are often fractured by voices coming from my parents' room next door.

'Over the top!' I hear my Dad shout. He repeats it over and over again, the panic rising with each repeat. It is almost thirty years since he was a sixteen-year old cowering in a trench in France, but the horror has never left him. His early life was a shambles: he was one of twelve children born to farm worker and master butcher Robert Matthews and his wife Emma in the Oxfordshire village of Grimsbury, later moving to Baginton, a village just outside Coventry, where he spent an unsupervised, wild and uneducated childhood. Robert drank, and the stories are hazy, lost in the past – but my Dad grew up in spite of it all, spending a lot of his growing up with various sisters of whom I know nothing.

At just twelve years old, he is sent to a farmer in Yorkshire, where he is treated like a slave. He is so unhappy that at sixteen, he gives a false age and joins the army like so many young men at this time. He never talks about it, and will avoid the subject with practised skill, though he makes the occasional exception. He talks once about the night he first did sentry duty, a boy of sixteen in a strange country. He heard a noise in the darkness, and called out, but the fear was so great that he disgraced himself by soiling his trousers. His shame is still fresh, and never leaves him. A boy in a violent and alien man's world, it is all too much. If I ever make a fuss about my food, he is always quick to tell me about how he ate ants and grubs in his jam.

Other legacies of his time in France also stay with him, much to the amusement of his family and the chagrin of my mother. He begins to sing one particular song, but is never allowed to finish it, as at the crucial point my mother shouts, '*Sam!*' in a commanding voice, and he stops. We never learn all the words to that song. He disappears, to the greenhouse or his shed, a twinkle in his mild blue eyes and a vague flick from his one hand.

In his shed, out comes the snuffbox, a small oval box

made from bone. He pushes it open with what is left of his thumb, takes a pinch and puts it into his nose. Somehow he manages to balance the tiny box on his knee without dropping it.

'Dirty old squaddie,' is my mother's remark as he comes back into the kitchen. She hates the habit, but cannot stop him.

Although he can hold his teacup with the elegance of a lady having tea at the vicarage, his favourite method is to pour some into his saucer and drink it with noisy slurps. This also provokes Mother into shouting 'Dirty old squaddie', but he remains impervious.

We begin to eat our dinner and Dad presents us with his teaser. 'Two ducks in front of a duck and two ducks behind a duck,' he says. 'How many ducks are there?'

'Five,' we reply.

'No, three,' he insists.

The argument continues throughout the meal, and is trotted out every week without fail. We never agree on the answer.

How wise we always are long after events have passed. I so often wish Dad were here now so that I could tell him just what a great man he was. Growing up, I criticise him constantly for so many things. No doubt influenced by my mother's irritation with him, I tell him off for the way he says things, for his snuff taking, never seeing the real man at all. He has some pretty awful habits, left over from a total lack of upbringing followed by years in the army. One such habit is spitting, or even worse, blowing his nose into the gutter. I am horrified when I see him do it, and always run home to tell my mother. She shouts at him, but it makes no difference, and there is a hurt look on his face when he calls me a telltale.

FROM PARADISE TO EDEN

Years later ,when I am working in the offices at Courtaulds, I ride behind him on my bike. He only has one arm, so turning right into Silverton Road is hazardous. It doesn't daunt my dad – he just simply goes! He can't signal, so he just turns and hopes for the best. This is the way my father approaches his whole life, by taking chances with no thought for the next moment. How he escapes an accident I shall never know, but being the prissy child that I am, I tell my mother. He should hate me, but all I ever know from him is unconditional love.

The rose that grows against a wall in our garden is trained with loving care by my dad. It is spring, so out come the rickety old wooden steps, and up he goes. Precariously balanced, his one arm reaching out with his one-handed shears, he gently prunes it back. The steps wobble, but somehow he remains on them.

'Sam – *get down*!' My mother's voice from the back doorstep.

'It's alright, Annie, them's as safe as 'ouses'.

My mother gives up and returns to her kitchen, rubbing her hands down her pinafore. This is just another way to show his defiance in the face of an uncertain life.

I am mortified when a fellow worker in the office tells me that my Dad is directing traffic in Lockhurst Lane. He is a works policeman, and he loves a drink. He has been in the pub at dinnertime – and there he is, directing the flow of traffic for all to see. How ashamed I am, and of course, I tell my mother.

My dad's drinking is a problem, which is kept in check by a game my parents play. Mum pretends that she doesn't know he has had a drink, he sucks mints and pretends that she doesn't know. As long as each one of them keeps up the pretence, he doesn't drink too much. His trips to the allotment are always long ones, as he visits the Red House or the Navvie on his way home. He is well known in both pubs, and in years to come I discover that my children were often left outside in pushchairs while Dad had a drink.

Trips on the bus into town are to be avoided if possible, as he always manages to embarrass me. On one occasion I go upstairs, Dad is downstairs. We arrive at the Swanswell stop and I know quite well where we are, so start to climb down the stairs.

'Come on, you silly mess' – his voice carries through the bus.

'Is that your father?' someone asks.

'No,' is my reply. It isn't the first time or the last that I disown him.

Whenever I am short of money, I waylay him on his way to or from work, and he always finds me something. He never bears a grudge on my tale-telling – just accepts it because in truth, he is a better person than I am. Dad's pocket rustling is always a sign for me to look hopeful. He rustles paper, smiles his secret smile, then produces a sweet, usually a humbug. It has bits of paper and fluff clinging to it, but I am quite happy to suck the bits off.

Mornings always begin with my Dad waking me up. If he has been on night shift, he comes into the bedroom, the stale smoky smell of the Time Office clinging to his navy blue uniform, pulls the curtains back and says, 'Wakey wakey, the sun is streaming over the housetops.' Even if it is pouring with rain, the greeting is always the same. In his hand there will be a half-melted Walls ice cream in its paper. He brings it home from work for me, so I begin the day with ice cream. At Christmas he puts a tot a whisky in my first cup of tea, carrying it up to me in bed. I know I shouldn't be having this, so it tastes really good.

No one can tell a story like my dad. He tells me about the time he was a boy in Baginton and visited a field day held in the grounds of Baginton Hall. While sitting on the wooden seat of the old privy, he saw a big table laid for a wedding banquet, and the bride and groom sitting at its head. As he watched in the late evening light, the wedding guests and bride with groom got up and slowly walked towards him. He was so afraid that he ran away with his trousers still around his ankles. What did my Dad see that day, I wonder? He isn't a man to make up stories, dealing always with facts.

He tells me too about the sewage works at Baginton, how the tomato seeds in the human waste take root and grow, and how he picks the tomatoes. This story is usually told as I eat my tea and it makes me shudder.

He is a great one for tricks, my dad, and even though he only has one arm, he is very dextrous with a penny. He shows me the penny, and he flicks it – and it disappears! He re-discovers it behind his ear, or in his trouser turn-up, and I never work out how he does it. My dad is magic. As my own children grow up, he plays games with them. Card games like snap; he cheats outrageously, we all know he is doing it, and he just smiles his roguish little boy's smile and carries on cheating. He makes them little paper boats, or aeroplanes, his one hand folding the paper expertly, showing them how to do it. They still remember the trick years after he has gone.

I do not always appreciate his playfulness, especially when he chases me and pushes the stump of his right arm into my face. He thinks this is funny, but it fills me with nightmare horrors. Worse still is the chase with his artificial arm. He never wears it, but it stands in a corner, pink and menacing, its long pink fingers curled inwards in a beckoning gesture. He takes great delight in chasing me with it, unaware of its journey through my mind and into my dreams.

Then there are his teeth, another source of fun to my dad. My children tell me when they are grown how, when he has had a drink, he nods off in his chair and his teeth, with a mind of their own, drop down onto his bottom lip.

Dad has been to the dentist, and I am a small girl waiting for him to come home. He will have called in to a shop, there may be a treat in a paper bag buried in the depths of his pocket. I wait at the top of the entry until I see him walking with that fast, slightly leaning gait of his. I run up to meet him, and he smiles at me. His mouth is full of huge white teeth with deep pink gums, and I am terrified. I cry and run away into the kitchen, and he is so puzzled. His face has a hurt look as I try later to explain my fear. Dad always had small teeth, and this new image is one of a stranger. This doesn't stop him from letting them drop and pushing them out with his tongue whenever he wants to shock, or when the seeds from my mother's fig and rhubarb jam get behind them.

'It's these seeds, Annie,' he complains, 'they get behind my plate.'

'Don't eat it then!' is always her reply.

Walking home from his job at Courtaulds is a voyage of discovery for him. He arrives in the kitchen holding dirty hankies, and once even an embroidered shawl. These articles he gives to my mother, who soaks them and washes them and we use them. He never misses a thing, and often says to me, 'When life gets rough, Dulc, just put your head down, keep going and watch one foot fall in front of the other.' He also tells me, 'It won't always be dark at six.'

He and my mother have a quotation for every situation. When I complain because my arm aches when helping to beat the batter for Sunday yorkshire pudding, my mother says, 'Your muscles will waste if you don't use them'. These sayings are a part of our life, a strong thread weaving the days and weeks together, giving a certain logic and meaning .

Losing things is my speciality; I forget things and lose them on a daily basis. My mother tells me 'Write it on your forehead with your finger before you go to sleep and you'll remember it in the morning'. It usually works, but if I really have lost something, my dad sits with me and tells me, 'Remember where you had it last'. Both these methods worked then, and they still do.

Dad has a 'Rattin' jacket; that's what he calls the old jacket that hangs on the back door. He loves his jacket, but my mother tries hard to lose it. He also has what he calls his 'hard hat' – a black bowler. When my mother gives them both to the Rag and Bone man he is heartbroken, and it remains an unspoken criticism between them for a long, long time.

At Christmas, we use the front room with its brown rexine couch and chairs. My mother buys balloons, our only decoration, and they are pinned into the corners. These balloons give more pleasure to my Dad than to any of us, as he takes them down, head butting them but not letting anyone get one away from him. As my own children grow, they too are put through the balloon game that gives him endless pleasure. He has, always, that childlike way of getting joy from simplicity.

It is at Christmas that I have my frightening experience, and it is Dad who consoles me while the others laugh. I have to go through the darkened middle room to reach the kitchen, and I hesitate, afraid of the dark. I pluck up courage and go into the room; as I cross it, I hear a voice, a loud hoarse whisper and it calls my name. I stop and say 'yes' – but the voice has gone and I am now terrified. I know I have heard it, but this is just 'our kid' imagining things again – but my Dad is there, comforting and protecting me. The favourite game we play is probably the cause of my terror. The card table is brought into the front room, and little bits of paper with the alphabet on are placed in a circle. This is called 'spirits'; we sit round, and place our little fingers lightly on the glass in the centre. Someone asks a question, and the glass mysteriously moves to each letter in turn, spelling out words. There is a lot of friendly argument as we do this.

'Our Myrt is pushing it.'

'I'm not, look, my finger is hardly on!'

The results are often very scary, and eventually my mother refuses to let us carry on. Her religion forbids future prediction, but she has a very strong sixth sense, an uncanny ability to 'see' things, so she struggles all her life with it. On this occasion we seem to be getting messages from a Jewish prisoner of war, and the game becomes very sinister. It is brought to a close when we are getting names and details that seem too real, so going through the darkened living room, I take the spirit with me, and I hear it.

My fear of darkness is real and terrible; I delay going to the outside lavatory at night until the very last minute, standing legs crossed by the back door.

'Just go!' my mother says.

'I'll take her.' This from my dad as always. He stands patiently outside in the cold, in the rain, just waiting until I am ready to make the run for the back door. Singing loudly while I am in there helps to see off the shadows, but knowing that my dad is outside the door is my security. No vampires or ghosts will get past him.

He is such a clever and patient man, never getting angry, though there must be many frustrations for him. He washes up, his one hand expertly swilling the crockery. He dries them, by sitting on the old stool and holding the cloth between his knees. He eats his food and no one thinks to cut up his meat, he would be so indignant. The scrambled eggs he makes are matchless. He sits, bowl between his knees to keep it still while he beats together eggs and milk, then piles the finished meal onto hot buttered toast, the butter thick enough to make teeth marks in. Someone in the street asks me how I help my dad, and I am surprised by the question. My Dad doesn't need any help, he can manage everything himself.' I reply. He spends hours in his shed making boxes by holding the wood in the vice. Using his stump to balance things, he makes work boxes for my mother, small perfectly jointed boxes for me, and not once do I marvel at the skill and patience it takes. Before I go to school I am told 'Clean your shoes, they are filthy!' Out comes the old stool, and Dad says, 'Put 'em up on here', and he cleans them. My mother complains that he is spoiling me, but it doesn't stop him.

His daily habits cause problems, yet he refuses to change them. We have no bathroom, so the 'Jeremiah' sits under the bed. My Dad's daily task is to bring it down, but for some reason known only to him, he leaves it halfway down the stairs. The stairway is dark, so without fail, my mother rushes down each morning and kicks it over.

It becomes a pantomime, a daily routine of crashing and shouting which always ends with Dad going to the allotment. He clears up first though, and I wonder why he leaves the booby trap to catch my mother, and also why she doesn't anticipate it!

Here we are, my dad and me, walking along a lane. The sun is shining and I am hot and tired. We are walking home from his sister's house – his sister Beatrice, the only one I ever get to meet. I am looking at the rooftops and telling him that the tiles are green. 'No, they're red' – 'No, green'. We continue to argue as we make our slow way home, but I am convinced that they are green. Why is this such a strong memory for me now – the easy banter, the heat, the timeless feeling of that summer afternoon and our argument about colour? Maybe because in a traumatic and lonely childhood, this memory is one of companionship and warmth with the man who was my father.

It is 1982, and I am living in Morecambe. The hotel I am running makes it very hard to get back to Coventry to see my parents, so the full burden of them falls upon my brother. Dad is frail, but when I go in he insists that I take him 'up the Wolfe'. He wants to go into the Sketchley shop where he gets his trousers altered. Today he wants them letting out. He is greeted with affection by the woman in the shop. She knows him well!

'Taking in again, Mr Matthews,' she says.

'Them keep fallin' down.'

She takes the trousers off him, but he hangs on to them.

'You'll need to measure me' – this said with a roguish smile.

Out comes the tape measure as she wraps it around his middle.

'You just want me to put my arms round you.' He smiles again, his face like a small boy who has just won a battle.

Just a week later I receive a phone call from my brother in Coventry.

'Dad's dead, Dulc,' he tells me. I am stunned; he was old, but somehow indestructable and I can't believe my brother's words.

'He still had his hand gripped round the brandy bottle, and he had a silly grin on his face.'

We talk about him, and my brother makes me laugh. Dad must have 'come over queer', as he used to say, and reached for the brandy which was strictly for medicinal purposes. We both hoped he had managed to drink some before his heart stopped forever.

He was eternally child-like in his fun and simplicity, accepting all the misfortunes and disillusionments of his life with courage. Truly, a man among men.

Chapter Fifteen

My mother is a handsome woman, austere and dignified. She doesn't seem to know how to give love. As an adult, I know that to the best of her ability she did, but here, as a child I am afraid, yet somehow challenged by her stern aloofness, which provokes defiance in me. My relationship with my mother is a complicated mix of love, the need to be loved, the fear of being unloved, and the fear of silence. I lurch between her sternness, wrath, silences and occasional softness. I cling to the gentle moments, clutching them to me in a desperate struggle to make them last. Sometimes, she calls me Dulch – these are the precious soft times; I hold them inside jealously, wrapping myself in them in preparation for their absence. Is all that I am the sum total of my relationship with my mother? Within its complex web there must be choices, scraps of the person who is me – my genetic inheritance and uniqueness.

As I think now of my mother, I see her in her kitchen. The kitchen is her own kingdom; here, she is in total charge, holding sway over the old gas cooker, the brick copper in the corner, and the contents of all cupboards. I enter at my peril because I get under her feet and meither her. I stand cautiously by the open back door and say, 'Can I have a piece of bread and jam please?'

'May I have…'

'Can I have…'

'*May* I have…!'

This exchange lasts for several minutes, my mother's voice rising in pitch at each repeat, until I say, 'I don't want one now anyway!' and run off to sulk in private.

Our kitchen is a large square room, its red stone floor always freshly scrubbed. Rag rugs made from old clothes make the floor look warmer. There is a black range on one wall, now out of use, with the small drop leaf table made by my one-armed dad standing against it. The old stool, also made by Dad, sits under the table, with a chair at each end. It is painted pale yellow, the glossy walls running with condensation on Mondays. A worktop under the window is where my mother does the cooking, and a big cupboard on the wall (another of dad's creations) holds her flour and other things like dried fruit in jars, and the dried figs I love so much. These are not to be touched as they are there in readiness for making fig and rhubarb jam.

Above the gas cooker is a wooden rack for the tea towels, and also odd bits like socks hanging to dry. There is no talk of fire hazards, but there is a fire, once. The hanging tea towels catch in the gas flame, fanned by an open back door. Yellow-orange flames flare suddenly upwards, licking greedily, devouring the towels as I watch silently, too fascinated to move. My brother Clive is now a fireman, and gives my mother a stern lecture about fire.

Mum lights the gas stove with tapers, and sometimes bits of tight rolled newspaper, which I am told I must never do. Joined to the kitchen is the pantry where the big deep white sink lives. This is the place where we have our strip wash to avoid dragging out the tin bath. When it is cold, a bowl of water is brought into the kitchen and a wash is had in front of the open oven door to snatch at some warmth. Washing is always a quick job in the winter, not to be lingered over.

I love the pantry with its high shelves full of things I mustn't touch. Dad has built a safe with a mesh door to keep the flies out and let air in. Mum keeps her perishables in here. The milk is brought in from the front step, often with holes in the cardboard tops where birds have pinched the cream. These are the days before refrigerators and freezers, so in summer, the huge jam kettle is filled with water, the milk bottles stood in it and covered with muslin. This helps to stop the milk from going sour, but sometimes it doesn't work. This is when my mother makes curd cheese. She puts the sour milk into muslin cloth and hangs it over the sink where it drips the whey into a bowl, leaving the curd. The process fascinates me, and I give the bag a furtive squeeze, just to help the process along.

My mother uses the red stone pantry floor to stand her big stew-pan on. Every Friday she gets bones from the butcher. She brings them home, puts them into a big pan with water, and simmers them for hours. This is the base for her stews that are our staple diet. Vegetables from the allotment are added with pearl barley, and we eat it for days, the changes created by adding dumplings or mashed potatoes. My mother is very proud of her 'stock pan', and sometimes she holds it upside down when it has gone cold, saying with pride, 'Look, solid jelly!' It doesn't always work, and on one occasion the contents plop onto the kitchen floor. I am silent – she might be angry. But she laughs as she scrapes it up, so today is a good day after all.

If I am quiet, I am allowed to watch her when she cooks. She is making the apple tart for Sunday, the pastry is expertly rolled and lifted, and I want so badly to do it too. Apples are peeled, the peel coming off in one long ribbon, dropping onto the enamel table top still in one long piece. The apples are gently simmered with sugar and cinnamon, then added to the pastry. It comes out of the oven lightly golden and encrusted with sugar, and is put into the safe until Sunday.

My mother lives in a continuous battle with her two selves. For whatever reason, she is a stern disciplinarian who makes no allowances for children or for illness. She loves music, but denies herself the pleasure of listening. She has a rich and lovely contralto voice, but doesn't allow herself to use it very often. She writes pages and pages of lectures on religion that remain in her bureau, unread until her death, and unheard by anyone.

In the years following her death in 1983, I take the memories of my gentle mother from my memory. Holding them tenderly like precious pearls, I look at them, treasure them, then return them to where they are safe, until I need them again.

Chapter Sixteen

Memory is stirred by smells, activated by taste. Roast lamb smells of Sunday, and it means Mum shouting at Dad because he isn't ready for the Christadelphian meeting. Roast lamb is followed by my mother's apple tart, the like of which I have never since tasted. My mother's apple tart is matchless, and though a good cook myself, I have still never made a tart that reaches her perfection.

After the meal, we clear away, and I watch as my father sits on the old stool, tea towel in his one hand as he patiently dries up the crockery.

Sunday afternoon is endless afternoon naps, Billy Cotton's band show on the wireless, and yawning boredom stretching through until teatime. Woe betide me if I make a sound, so I study my mother's sleeping face, mentally tracing the deep lines from nose to mouth, and the way her head falls to one side making her mouth droop at the corners. I watch the birds from the window, becoming mesmerised by the movement of the silver birch tree in the breeze, and I make up stories in my head. I study the fly-paper hanging from the upturned glass light shade, watching the flies as they touch it, struggle and then become still. There are lots more in the upturned shade.

The grandmother clock strikes four, and Dad makes a cup of tea. Purgatory is over now until the evening when Bible readings begin. My own children, and their children, all had a bedroom haven of books and toys. Going to their room was not a penance. I do not retreat to my bedroom (unless sent there in disgrace) because it is cold and without character. My books are few, no games or toys. It is a cheerless place to be endured with stoicism. So, I sit through the sleeping and the bible reading because at least it is warm in the sitting room.

Cooking is, I think, a job my mother enjoys. She is usually content in her kitchen, and my pleasure is to stand – not too close – and watch her. Sometimes she sings as she bakes, her deep rich contralto voice is lovely to hear. If I am really lucky, I will be given a lump of butter rolled in sugar, or a stick of rhubarb and a saucer filled with sugar. Then I wander into the garden to enjoy my treat. A real treat is a spoonful of condensed milk, so I hang around the kitchen, ready for scraps and tit-bits that may come my way.

I have become fussy with my food, playing about with it and refusing to eat. To tempt me, my mother makes potato mountains and gravy rivers. Coming home from school in winter, I am occasionally sat in the big armchair by the fire with a board across the arms. Then I have apple sandwiches sprinkled with brown sugar, and bread pudding hot and crusty on top. On Tuesdays, when my mother has been into town with Aunt Maud, I get a kunzle cake. This is a chocolate cup filled with sponge and cream and wrapped in cellophane paper.

The glory hole in the corner of the kitchen has a strange smell, a mixture of polish, gas and musty corners. It is very dark in here, but I creep in to fetch my mother's button box. The box is filled with buttons taken from every old garment before the material is re-used either for rugs or dusters. I tip them out onto the stone floor, run my fingers through them allowing them to trickle onto the red tiles, sorting them into piles. There is something so comforting about their familiarity. The tiny pearl buttons taken from Dad's shirts, round red ones like cherries that used to be on my summer dress, and the shiny brass ones from Dad's works jacket, or are they from something my brother wore? I arrange and rearrange the buttons, telling myself stories as they sit in their lines on the floor. In the years to come, the buttons are sorted by my daughter and by my sons, then, in turn by my grandchildren, before they vanish into the past; all those magic buttons, each with its own story.

My mother is two people. She talks to me sometimes about her time as a child. The middle one of seven, she has a poor childhood and, despite her siblings, a lonely one. She tells me how she used to dance in the street to the hurdy-gurdy man as he slowly turns the handle of his barrel organ. She is clever – she loves to read, and though her schooling ends when she is twelve, she manages to get from somewhere a volume of Shakespeare's sonnets which she hides away to read secretly. Her two older brothers laugh at her and call her a blue stocking. Her father, my grandfather, is an old soldier, strict and severe. He is a Christadelphian, and his religion rules her life just as it rules mine in my childhood. She is afraid of her father, and tells me how she is forbidden to look into a mirror. To do that is the sin of vanity.

So it is with me; looking into mirrors and admiring one's reflection is not to be done – it is wrong. My mother's youngest sister Maud is pretty and helpless in a feminine way, and so escapes much of the severity doled out to my mother, who is self-willed and headstrong, standing up to her father though she fears him. She tells me of her mother, my grandmother. Grandmother Sarah Durnford was born in a village named Durnford in Wiltshire. Details of her life are hazy to my mother, but as she talks, a fascinating picture emerges of a warm cheerful mother, an austere father, and poverty. Of two brothers who had to strip to the waist even in the coldest winters, and wash under the water pump in the yard. My mother loved her brother Bert, who was, it seems, a loveable, charming and wayward youth. She talks about how he rides the farmer's cow around the field, and steals an apple pie from someone's open window. Bert is sent to America, where he marries, has a child, and goes into the army in 1914. He is killed on the last day of the war in 1918. This is also the year that my mother's favourite sister Nancy dies in the influenza epidemic.

Her upbringing creates a rigid framework upon which she builds her own values and beliefs. She marries because this is what you do in 1924, but she always resents her marriage and her children. In a different time she would be an academic, a career woman, so her children are merely tolerated. They are an intrusion, an irritation to be dispensed with quickly. Myrtle is the first to arrive, followed two years later by Clive. There is a gap of ten years before I arrive in 1937, and I am her Gethsemane. I do not understand what this means, but I do understand that I am a nuisance, an irritation. I talk too much and ask too many questions. I dream too much and have too many nightmares. 'I didn't want you,' she tells me often. My sister is lovely, she has dark hair and green eyes. Aunt Lou, my mother's older sister, loves Myrtle and Clive, but finds me, if she sees me at all, a rather silly dreamy child. My mother introduces me to the people at 'The meeting' in the Christadelphian hall. 'This is Dulcie, she is my plain one...' As I get older I understand that plain just means not pretty like Myrtle, but when I talk to my big sister she tells me that my mother always introduced *her* as the plain one, so I am confused.

As an adult, I cross the city to visit her on two buses with a baby, a small girl, a pushchair and large bag, to be told at the gate, 'You can't come in, I'm far too busy'. So I make the long trek home again feeling hurt and rejected, yet never angry with her, and I don't know why.

The other person, who is also my mother, is gentle, and I pull up the tuffet to sit between her knees. The tuffet is a little pouffe with a crochet cover. If I pull it towards her and she smiles, I know it's alright to sit down. In these soft moments, she brushes my hair and tells me stories. She has a little book of poems with a date inside '1914', and she reads them to me. Each word is held in my mind, turned around and savoured with delight. 'I'm losted! Could you find me please!'

> *Poor little frightened baby.*
> *The wind has tossed her golden fleece,*
> *The stone has scratched her dimpled knees.*
> *I stooped and lifted her with ease.*
> *And softly whispered 'Maybe'.*

The poem makes me cry, and this once I am not laughed at. As a woman, I read it to my children. The pages of the book, now faded and brown, are falling out of their place, crackly like dry autumn leaves. They crumble as I turn the pages.

This soft mother tells me stories about the blue butterfly slides as she pins them into my hair. I allow her to pull at the tangles because I want to hear the end of the story. It is Spring, and the flowering currant bush is full of little pink clusters. My mother picks one and tucks it into my hair ribbon because it matches the pink of my dress. She lets me brush her long hair, so I sit behind her, plaiting and twisting the thick strong grey/silver strands. When I have finished, she winds it into rolls around her head with the wooden peg kept in the hair box in the pantry. She wears her hair like this until the day she dies, but I love it when it is brushed down, because then, she looks soft and gentle.

We listen to the wireless together at teatime, and I am absorbed by 'Anne of Green Gables'. I am taught to knit, struggling because of my left-handedness. The art mastered, I now do fair-isle patterns with scraps of wool left over from my mother's knitting. My mother knits me a fair-isle tammie which I wear with pride. We spend time together learning how to tie bows. Because of my left handed problem, I find this very hard, but I manage eventually, even though they do slide undone again. I like my buttoned shoes the best because then I can use the silver button-hook.

Why do all mothers clean their children's faces with spit on a hankie? I hate it when my mother does it; she spits on the corner of her lace hankie and wipes my mouth. I shout, 'Let *me* lick it', and I shudder with distaste, but she still does it. My own children now accuse me of the same habit, so I must have done it too.

When I am almost nine years old, my world suddenly and abruptly changes. My mother has collapsed, and my sister stands with me as ambulance men carry her out on a stretcher. I am devastated; she must be dead. No-one tells me what has happened. My sister, newly married, is left with the task of looking after me and my Dad, and my dad is being difficult because he is lost without my mum. Myrtle and Dad fall out, shouting at each other, but I still don't know where my mother is. I get upset, sobs shaking me and sending my words out jerkily towards any-one who will listen.

We run out, my sister and I, my dad following us and shouting. We run to Eden Street where Myrtle's husband's mother lives, and we sit around a big table drinking tea from huge mugs. I am still sobbing, and now they laugh at me. 'Our Dulc is a regular drama queen,' they say. But my mother is dead and my dad is angry, which he never is, so I am frightened.

Then I discover that my mother isn't dead, but is in hospital, so I can go and see her. Myrtle finds funny red blotches all over my tummy, and paints them with gentian violet. My tummy looks wonderful, covered in purple spots, so I lift up my dress to show my mother. Myrtle is horrified and I am quickly covered up, but I don't know what the fuss is about. I start having tantrums. Poor Myrtle, just twenty with a new husband, and she has to cope with a little girl and an awkward father. She doesn't do my hair properly, so I have a tantrum. Myrtle's husband Len tries to make me laugh. He rolls up his trouser legs and does a ballet dance for me. I am holding a stemmed glass, and I get so excited that I crush it in my hand.

Chapter Seventeen

My life is a series of confusions and fear. The air-raid shelters have gone, the war is over, leaving us with falling walls and ration books, and now my mother goes away, leaving me with a dad who suddenly stops knowing what to do and a sister who finds me a handful.

There is a thread of fantasy that helps me to make sense of my life. I find it in the hours spent listening to the wireless. 'The Secret Garden' is a real place. My mind paints such pictures; I am *in* the secret garden; I can see an old wooden gate set into a big stone wall, hear it creak as it opens after being hidden for a long time. There are new shoots pushing their way upwards through dead leaves, and tiny spiders, undisturbed for years, being turfed out from their cosy cobweb corners. It smells damp and earthy, tangled brambles cover the ground. Moss clings to ancient stone walls. Then there is a poem read to us at school that captivates me. ''The green glass beads' and its goblins... I close my eyes and see light shining in the green glass beads, feel the smoothness of the beads as they slide through my fingers.

'Nymph, nymph, what are your beads?
Green glass goblin, why do you stare at them?
Give them me.
No.
Give them me, give them me.

No.'

I recite the words to my mother, saying them over and over again – and she listens!

On very special occasions we listen to Charlie Kunz on the wireless. He plays the piano, and his easy style makes such a lasting impression on me. But these times are only with the gentle mother and she doesn't stay for long at all.

When I am eight years old and I have recovered from having my tonsils and adenoids out, we go away for the only holiday of my childhood. I am still more fortunate than my brother and sister, as they never have one at all. I go with my mother to the Paradise post office and watch Mr Beer count out sixty pounds into her hand. We get up while it is still dark, and a car comes to collect my mother, my father and me. Silently, because for once I am lost for words, I watch the sun rise as we drive along, and I think it is the most wonderful sight I have ever seen. We go to Devon, and stay in a hotel that is reached by climbing up two hundred and forty stone steps. There are beech trees overhanging the steps that drop their leaves onto us. I collect tiny beech nuts as we climb.

Being in the hotel is lovely, and I enjoy the attention of Nora. Nora is a nurse and she thinks I am such a nice polite little girl, so I learn that behaving in a certain way makes me more acceptable. We go to Brixham and get onto a boat. As this is such a new experience I am again awed into silence. Nora has bought me a tiny brooch, it's a little black dog and it is pinned onto my brown dress. I lean over the side of the boat – and watch as my little brooch falls down, down into the deep dark water, and I cry with such an intensity of feeling. It has gone forever and I love it so much.

Aunt Maud. My mother's sister, is married to Uncle Ralph who is my dad's brother. We go to Aunt Maud's house every week. Aunt Maud keeps hens, and I think she looks a lot like them. She has this way of putting her head onto one side and clucking as she talks to my mother. 'Ooh our Sarah' she seems to say a lot. Then they both laugh, deep waves of laughter that make tears run down their cheeks. I help to feed the hens, following aunt Maud down the garden path. She 'clucks' to the hens, calling them to her, and I am allowed to feed them too, enjoying the feel of their beaks as they peck the seed from my hand. Aunt Maud makes 'mash' for them with potato peelings. It has a lovely oaty smell when I stir it.

Uncle Ralph is a gentle man, like my dad. In his trouser pocket he always has Mintoes, the rustle of paper telling me that a treat is in store. He works for the railway, his big dapple grey horse with hairy hooves, pulling the dray. His horse is his pride and joy; the soft grey coat is brushed and the mane untangled and braided. Just once, Unc' sits me on his back, the ground looking such a long way away that I almost stop breathing. When we go the Walsgrave show, we ride on the dray, and I can see the horse's tail trimmed with ribbons. His mane is plaited with ribbon too, and Unc' is very proud if him.

Do memories always recall only sunshine? These long, seemingly endless afternoons of warm hay and sunshine, the smell of horses mingling into hay, voices blending with smells, as sounds become fainter and fainter, until I fall asleep where I sit, to be carried home by my dad or by Unc', and put to bed without ever waking up properly.

It is summer, and I am in Kenilworth with my mother and Aunt Maud. We are staying in the house of one of 'the brethren', Mr Islip Collier, who has written a book about

God. My mother and Aunt Maud sit in the big room drinking tea, so I idle the time away outside. This is nothing like home; here, there is grass, lots of it, and it is very quiet. I sit on the grass and pick daisies, stringing them together in a long chain. Happy in my own company, alone yet not lonely, I talk to my imaginary friend, sharing secrets as I make daisy chains.

Today we go to see Mrs Critchley, who is a 'sister' from the brethren. She is such a lovely lady, small and pretty with a warm smile. She is very pleased that my mother has brought me to see her, and gives me a tiny crinoline lady made out of sugar. We also bring home some old clothes that go into the trunk in the back bedroom. Dresses made of satin and trimmed with black braid. The crinoline lady is my delight; I cradle her all the way back home along the Stoney Stanton road. When I get home, I decide to wash her as she is very dusty, and as the water closes over her, she dissolves, her colours slowly fading as she becomes smaller, her features disappearing, the frills on her gown turning to a doughy stickiness. I am devastated! My crinoline lady disappears from my hands, and I cry as I cried when my brooch fell into the water. Nothing that is beautiful it seems, lasts.

Pem Harold is another friend called 'sister' by my mother, and we go to see her in her little shop on the corner of Peel Street. I am told to call her Mrs Harold because small girls must never use grown-ups christian names. Mrs Harold gives me an iced lolly that she has made. And it lasts me all the way back home, running down my arm and onto my dress.

My mother's 'soft' times are very special. One such day she takes me for a walk to Miller's brook. Henley road is the only place where we can find any green grass apart from the tiny square in our back garden, so this is a special trip. We sit by the little stream, then wander across to a fallen log. My mother gazes out at nothing, while I plan a tea party. I know that there will never be a tea party, but I get pleasure from dreaming about what I will make for tea and who will come to my party. We make lists, and I wish so much that this mother would stay and that I could really have a tea party.

My mother will sometimes read my tea-leaves. I swill the dregs of tea around my cup three times and empty them into the saucer. She then studies the patterns in the bottom and tells me my fortune. We make this a game, because to forecast the future is against her religion, yet she loves to do it. She reads the cups for my Aunt Lou, but it is Aunt Lou who brings the 'game' to a final end. My mother somehow sees things, and Aunt Lou backs horses on the strength of them. When the horses start winning, my mother becomes afraid of her sixth sense, and refuses to do it again. In later years I can occasionally persuade her to do it just for fun, but it is always with reluctance.

Chapter Eighteen

Our lives are governed by, punctuated by the sayings of my parents. Every occasion is marked by a saying. My father breaks wind, and my mother tells me that *her* mother used to say 'If theest did break where theest did crack John, theest be two little men'. My grandmother came from Wiltshire so she said things in a different way. If I stand at the kitchen door arguing with my mother I say,'I won't…' 'Thee bist,' is her answer. We argue like this for a long time before I tire of the game and run off. I complain that I need new shoes, and my mother says, 'I met a man who complained that he had no shoes, until he met a man with no feet.' 'But if he had no feet, he wouldn't need any shoes,' I say. I am feeling sad, and my dad says, 'It won't always be dark at six' – or my mother says 'There was only one old woman ever got stuck, and they pulled her through.'

Someone is waiting for their baby to be born and I hear my mother say, 'An apple will fall from the tree when it's ready.' Like many mothers, she tells me to 'take off my coat inside the house, or I won't feel the benefit'. Her most obscure saying is when I am moving too slowly, then she tells me, 'It's like a frog's march to the dusthole'. I turn this one over in my mind trying to see why I am like a frog. I have an accident, and I hear 'Worse things happen at sea', or I am worried and she says 'The darkest hour is before dawn'. I over-reach myself and am told

'Cut your coat according to your cloth'. My mother is pleased with something, and she says, 'Although I say it as shouldn't...' The list is without end, and in years to come, when my parents have both died, my brother and I hold conversations in these sayings. He says to me as he goes, 'Remember the old woman Dulc', and it brings me comfort.

Watching my mother through the crack in her bedroom door, I try to fathom out her underclothes. She puts a pink thing called a corset around her middle, then pulls the laces in very tight. Then, she hooks her bust bodice onto the corset and covers it all up with silk bloomers. The procedure takes a long time, so I creep silently away before getting caught, but I am puzzled, and hope that when I am big I won't have to wear such awful things.

It is now 1985 and my mother has been dead for three years. I am in Morecambe when she dies, and the reality of her not 'being' takes a long time to sink in. In an unguarded moment, I remember – the tears gush from a deep inner place...

'I thought of you today, Mum. It was raining and we had been round the corner to Gladdings and the Paper shop. We walked back along the Stoney Stanton road arm in arm. I could see the twinkle in your brown eyes and your straight proud back. Up the entry, through the gate to be showered by raindrops from the forsythia, in the back door, into the back room warm and cosy. Green carpet, your chair and dad's chair and the old black couch. Beige curtains with spots on, though I can't remember the colour of the spots – were they green? Dad makes coffee in the white china cups with the gold rims, and we sit down to crusty batches (the Coventry way to say bread rolls) chelsea buns and coffee. I can see the silver birch from the window, the ivy climbing up the line post, the crooked crazy paved path. My eyes fill with tears, and suddenly I am crying for you, for all the lost opportunities, things unsaid. I want to stand before you and say so many things, but most of all, I want to hold you in my mind as the gentle mum, to remember the things about you that made me love you despite the hurt and the silences.'

We must all go through these emotions, it is a necessary part of the journey to who we eventually become – the shaping of the metal in the hot fire, the final serving of he umbilical cord. But the scars are long in healing.

Chapter Nineteen

In an insecure, noisy and frightening world, food marks the passing of time. Days are sentences, punctuated by breakfast, dinner and tea. This is the framework upon which I hang the cloth of my life. No matter how bad the dreams, morning always arrives with the reliable smell of toast smothered in dripping and the rich brown jelly at the bottom of the basin.

Porridge bubbles in the saucepan, tiny craters rising then exploding. I pour the glutinous contents into my dish, smothering it in brown sugar and the top of the milk.

Each morning the milkman leaves us two bottles of milk on the step, and each morning I hear my mother complaining that 'the blue tits have been at it again'. They neatly peck a hole in the cardboard top and drink off the cream. I don't think she really minds because she loves the birds. On the laburnum tree outside the back sitting room window, she hangs bags of nuts and lumps of suet. Dad goes up the garden path with breadcrumbs every day, calling to the birds as he scatters the bread. An old can filled with water is kept on the path and used to deter cats. If he sees an unsuspecting cat, he runs up the path, his stump quivering as he aims the water accurately in the cat's direction.

As my mother cooks at midday, when I move on to Grammar school, my dinner is warmed up on a saucepan of steam. This makes it very un-appetising, even though her cooking is good. This is more than compensated for by the occasional suppers, when my Mother bakes big potatoes in their skins, and we eat them salted and dripping in butter.

On Saturday, pocket money day, I go to 'Sid's shop' for liquorice wood sticks or sherbert. Sometimes both, the pleasure being in dipping the liquorice wood into the sherbet before chewing it. Sid Warner also sells sterilised milk, which is sometimes bought as a 'special'. We call it 'Sid's milk', the name giving my children of the future much amusement. Mrs Crabtree who lives in Eden Street makes cinder toffee. For threepence she gives us the slabs of golden honeycomb wrapped in greaseproof paper. We take it onto the crater in Crabmill Lane where we sit and eat it, separating it from the sticky paper, licking our fingers and wiping them down skirts, trousers and coats.

It is winter, and frost has made the ground very hard. 'It's time to pick the sprouts our Dulc' says my Dad, so we go to the allotment with a big shopping bag. I start at one end of the row, but the frost has made the sprouts hard to pull off and my fingers get so cold I cannot feel them. Still, we keep picking, because I have two hands and my Dad only has one. Arriving home with the Christmas sprouts, my hands begin to tingle as they warm up again.

Christmas tea is memorable; the table is spread with its special cloth of white linen embroidered with crinoline ladies in each corner. Then my mother brings in red salmon from the tin, ham from the tin, lettuce, cucumber and tomatoes, and thin slices of white bread, buttered and cut diagonally. There is always orange jelly with mandarin slices set into it, and the ultimate treat – evaporated milk or even tinned thick cream to follow. In years to come, my mother makes tea for my son and daughter, and they too recall mandarin oranges set in orange jelly.

No matter how I try to reproduce the flavour and the smell of these suppers, nothing ever comes anywhere near them. Is it, I wonder, because these were the days of innocence, of little responsibility? Time has the knack of softening the bad memories, the boredom, the sadness and frustration, and highlighting those stored gems that live again when they are evoked by a sudden smell, or a word. I can still find comfort in a baked potato or a dish of macaroni cheese. Not served cordon bleu with fancy trimmings, but just as it was, on my lap, by the fire. My security blanket when life becomes too much.

Chapter Twenty

Childhood in the thirties and forties is a precarious business. Remedies for all my ills are to be found in the folklore of my grandparents, whom I never knew. I am told that my Grandmother was disowned when she married my grandfather because he was a soldier and 'beneath' her. My mother talks of parcels arriving at Christmas when she is a little girl. They are full of clothes and food, sent to my grandmother by her two sisters, but they are returned because my grandmother Sarah Durnford is too proud to accept charity.

Illnesses are treated with old Wiltshire remedies, no doctors needed. For constipation it is necessary for the sufferer to sit on the Jeremiah which is filled with hot water. I stand up after agonising moments with a bright red, sore bum, and I *still* have constipation. When I do manage to 'go', my mother cheers and tells me to 'stick a flag in it and send it to Baginton'. This is where the sewage works are. The place where my father tells me he picks tomatoes grown from the seeds of excrement. How many of these tales to believe, I am not sure, but they pepper the pages of my growing with interest.

Colds are my winter nightmare. I catch them easily and they always 'go to my chest', my mother says. 'Our Dulcie's got a cold on her chest again,' she tells my father. I have a look, but I can't see anything there. It still means that I am smothered in Vick and a red flannel is pinned to my vest. It itches and smells and I hate it, though not as much as I hate the face steaming. Menthol crystals are put into a bowl of boiling water and my head is shoved over them, with a towel wrapped so tight around my head that I cannot breathe. Just like my bum, my face emerges red and sore, but I still can't breathe through my nose. My mouth stays open permanently, so I have to have my tonsils and adenoids out.

Colds leave me with earache because I have abscesses in them. I cry all night, and this is the only time I can remember being taken into my mother's bed. She wraps a hot water bottle in a cloth, and I lie with it against my ear. Eventually the abscess bursts, so then my mother warms olive oil and pours it into my ears to clean them out.

The cold remedy that I enjoy is the one my mother makes by mixing vinegar and honey with a drop of brandy. She sits me in front of the fire and puts the cup into my hand. It warms me to my toes, and I go to bed feeling better.

Cut knees and rashes are treated by a variety of methods, but they usually include calamine lotion, gentian violet or iodine. The iodine is bright yellow and stings so much it makes my eyes run, but the gentian violet is nice.

My mother says I must go to the dentist. We go on the bus into town and walk through Pool Meadow to the clinic. We are early, so we keep walking around and looking at the big clock in the bus station. When we arrive at the clinic, I am already afraid if this big event. We sit on the hard metal chairs with the other children and their mothers, and we wait for our turn. I can hear shouts and crying from the room where the man with the white coat is. It is my turn; we walk into the room and they sit me in a big chair that tilts me backwards. I open my mouth and the man in the white coat puts something in my mouth. My fear is now so great that all decorum goes to the winds, and I struggle out of the chair to run screaming all the way along Gulson road. My mother is mortified! I am taken home in disgrace, and my teeth stay untreated for many years to come. Tumpy, the ugly brass dog bought for me by my mother from the market, my prize for 'being good', has become my symbol of shame. Tumpy continues to remind me of what a dreadful little girl I am when I have a tantrum and throw him at my Dad. I miss, but Tumpy makes a big hole in the wall, which is left for a long time to remind me of my disgrace.

My tantrums are severe and often as I grow up. They stem from frustration and my mother's refusal to listen to me, or even acknowledge that I am there. They manifest on buses when I am ordered to sit somewhere, or in my room when I am shut up there for long periods of time. They frighten me, but I cannot stop them. I hurl myself from the sitting room, getting just out of reach before I shout '*I don't care!*' as I run up the stairs to throw myself sobbing, onto the bed.

Illness becomes useful as I move on to Grammar school. It is a way of avoiding unbearable things like being in the school play, or playing hockey and tennis. I have achieved the art of creating a high temperature so that I can be sent to the sick room. I get so good at this that I am sent home in a taxi. Now I will be in trouble; my mother doesn't believe in illness. 'Illness is weakness,' she tells us often. She is never ill, so I am not allowed to be. I ask the taxi driver to drop me at the end of Silverton Road, and I disappear across the common to kick my heels until home-time. Better to walk by the canal and pick poppies than face the unfaceable.

Chapter Twenty-one

There is a gap, a bridge of time stretching between me and my siblings. They are ten and twelve years old respectively when I am born. My mother, ashamed of her pregnancy, hides beneath a coat, going out in the evening to avoid being seen. As I am born in August, her discomfort must have been great. This is 1937; children are not aware of the mechanics of babies. So, my brother and sister live their lives, blissfully unaware of the shock to come. They have had my mother exclusively, not knowing that soon, they would have a cuckoo in the nest. They go off with Aunt Maud, and my mother goes into Gulson Road hospital, where I am born on the glorious twelfth. I am born with the cord still around my neck, struggling to breathe, yet determined to be born. Looking back across the years, I notice that there are many occasions when I struggle to get air into my lungs, as if living itself is a supreme effort.

When my mother returns home again, she has brought with her this small creature, crying and demanding attention constantly. My brother is very unhappy. Myrtle, being older, quite likes the baby, though the pleasure diminishes as I grow, and she finds herself taking me with her to meet her boyfriends!

In spite of the initial shock, as I begin to crawl and chatter, my brother plays games with me. We are on the dark, steep stairs; we are playing a game, and I tell him 'do it papperly'. He throws me into the air and I am terrified. This, though, is another game and it makes my dad laugh. He can't join in because he only has one arm, but Clive is young and strong.

I am totally in awe of my big brother. His presence in a room fills it, leaving no room for anyone else. He is dark, black hair and brown eyes, and his voice is deep and strong.

There are gaping holes in our childhood relationship, caused by the war. Clive is evacuated not long after the Coventry Blitz of 1940, and when I am still only eight years old, he leaves to go into the army. Myrtle has left two years before, so at eight, I am an only child.

Clive has lots of friends, all big and noisy, who come and go throughout my early years. I lie in bed on hot summer evenings and listen to their voices and their laughter. Feeling excluded from their banter, I kneel at the window so that no one will see me. My chin rests on the window sill as I listen, longing to be downstairs. He has a friend named Nick Dickson, who has a streak of white hair running through the dark. My mother seems to like Clive's friends, and I wonder why she doesn't like mine.

My brother is a presence of energy, a vital source of life filling every corner of the house. When he goes, a light goes out, the house becomes old and tired. He washes to go out for the evening, stripping to the waist and filling the stone sink in the pantry with steaming water. As he washes, he sings. His voice is deep and big too, and I stand in the kitchen listening.

'Where the blue of the night meets the gold of the day' or 'Mammy, mammy...' When he sings this one, he bends down on one knee and sings it to me. This makes me very happy. I adore this big brother. He sings a lot, Al

Martino is one of his favourites, so his washing is often accompanied by 'Here in my heart', but I like Al Jolsen the best.

His hair is black and shiny. It falls in a wave over his forehead, and if he is in a good mood, I am allowed to comb it and put grips in it. My mother lets me brush her long grey-black hair too, but the privilege of playing with Clive's hair out-shines everything.

Like all big brothers, he loves to tease me. I am good to tease because I scream and make a fuss, which seems to amuse everyone. My treasured doll, Christina Rossetti, is sitting on the dust-bin, and Clive is catapulting stones at her. I cry very loudly, and though no harm has come to her, I never forget this incident, and guard her very closely afterwards.

Clive has a motor-bike; a big roaring engine which excites me. I long to have a ride on it, but riding round with a kid sister on the pillion isn't the thing. He gets lots of speeding fines that he displays on the wall of his bed-room. I ask if he will give me a ride to school, as arriving to school on a motor-bike would be wonderful. He agrees, but charges me sixpence! When we are adults, we sit and talk into the night about all these things. He denies them all – we laugh together, but I remember very well!

Music is my passion, but there is no way of hearing it. I hear something on the wireless called Scherezade, but my mother switches it off and I am left with the longing to hear more. Clive plays opera records in the front room and I sit outside to listen. The music brings to me an intensity of feeling I never knew was possible before. When I am in my early teens, Clive takes me to the Central Hall to hear a live orchestra. I feel so grown up even though I am very afraid of doing the wrong thing. This is the most wonderful moment of my whole young life, leaving me with a longing to hear more and more. The feeling never leaves me.

It is Christmas; the fire has been lit in the front room, and the table is laid with the special cloth in the back room. I still have the tablecloth, with its crinoline ladies embroidered in each corner. On the table my mother has put a candle, and I am so impressed when Clive passes his hand through the flame. I ask him to do it again, and then – I try. When my hand burns I am puzzled, and Clive is reprimanded for showing a little girl such a trick.

After our tea, Christmas moves into the front room, where my Dad plays with balloons in the corner. As it gets later, and everyone is sleepy, my big brother tells me the ghost stories. We are sitting in the flickering glow of the fire, there are bits of paper lying everywhere, and discarded presents on the floor. The balloons lie unattended in a corner, and I sit by my brother's feet as he talks. His voice is soft and mysterious as he tells me about the leeches in the swamp. They crawl slowly, nearer and nearer, and he makes the wonderful sucking slurping noises of their slimy trail towards the house. I hold my breath; I am wonderfully, deliciously afraid. I run up to my cold dark bedroom quickly, and hide underneath the covers to dream of leeches and swamps.

On other evenings he tells me the story of Marley's ghost and the ghosts of Christmas past, present and future. I lie in my dark room and hear chains clanking up the stairs. Then I hear moans, such terrible moaning and clanking that I shake in terror under the covers. My bedroom door opens, and there is my brother. He has a chain in his hand, and he is laughing so much he can't stop. My mother is laughing too, but it takes a long time for me to sleep when they go again.

My big sister is happy and beautiful. Her hair is black and curly, her skin seems almost transparent and her eyes are green. She sings too, and her voice is clear, with a quality I only recognise in adulthood as being perfect. She plays the piano and sings 'Catari' and 'Come back to Sorrento'. Like my brother, her presence in my young life is important and far too fleeting. I am drawing, colouring in on a piece of scrap paper, and Myrtle helps me. She draws a lovely lady in a green dress, but I am so jealous that I scribble it out. My mother is horrified, and I am ashamed of my display of emotion. What a horrible little girl I am made to feel. Myrtle does everything so much better than I can.

She takes me out a lot when I am small. I have never been to the cinema, and when my sister wants to take me to the pictures to see 'Bambi', my mother tries to stop her, but Myrtle wins. Bambi's mother is killed, and Bambi stands alone in the forest. I am devastated! I cry very loudly, I can't stop, and Myrtle has to bring me home

She takes me to Birmingham and we go to Lewis's. This is a fairyland, and I am so excited. There are baboons in a big cage, and when I get home I tell my mother about the baboons with the big red bums. At times like these, they all laugh at me and I don't mind at all, though I never really understand what makes them laugh.

Myrtle goes into the ATS; She is stationed in Edinburgh at the castle, and she drives the officers about. When she comes home on leave, she tells me how she watches the soldiers parading in their kilts on polished brass, to see whether they have pants on underneath. I listen open-mouthed, and never know whether it is true or not.

When she comes on leave it is wonderful. I go with my mother to meet her at the bus station, and watch her running towards us. Her hat is perched on the side of her black curls, and she runs to meet us looking so bright and pretty. She laughs and sings, calling me Maybelle; and she brings me little presents...

When I get into the last class of the junior school I seem to always be in trouble. Each time it is my sister, my champion, who goes to see Mr Wills on my behalf. By now she is married and living in Canal Road, so I go there a lot in my teens. She is my haven and my support through troubled years. Stephanie and Robert grow up there, and I grow with them. The budgie sits in a cage in the big kitchen, listening to the daily fights as Myrtle gets Robert ready for school. Myrtle screams at Robert, and the budgie hops up and down on his perch shouting, 'Little bugger, little bugger'. She has a kettle that whistles. She shouts, 'Turn the bloody kettle off', but it isn't the kettle this time, it's Harding, her white cat and she is standing on his tail! Harding sits on the window-sill wanting to come in, and if we don't let him in, he closes one eye and stares. 'He does it on bloody purpose,' says my sister.

Her house is a cul-de-sac, and Alfred Herberts factory is at the bottom. Robert is learning to use a potty, so he takes it out into the street to use it, and my sister has to carry it back – full – to the cheers of the workmen pouring out at lunch-time. In later years when I am married and expecting my first baby, my husband is in the army, so I spend my time with my sister. In a house a few doors away live Mr and Mrs Glasgow and their little girl Lorraine. They are from Jamaica, and they share the house with other people also from Jamaica. Mr Glasgow has a party, and I go with Myrtle. Such a happy room full of laughing people. Mr Glasgow plays his guitar and sings a calypso verse to everyone in the room. He sings one to my unborn baby, telling me it will be a girl and that she will bring me much happiness. He was right. Then they hold a pole and keep lowering it as the men limbo underneath it. I go home at last with memories that will stay with me forever, of simple pleasure and warm friendly people.

Stephanie is ill when she is a baby, and we think it was meningitis. It leaves her damaged, so that she doesn't learn to walk until she is five years old, and she can't learn things. She is so gentle and sweet, with huge innocent blue eyes. My mother adores her, and Myrtle is very protective. I spend a lot of time with Stephanie, as she is only ten years younger than I am. She is about two years old when I take her for a walk across the common by the canal. I am talking to my friend Doreen, dreaming as usual, and I leave the pushchair unattended. Stephanie calls out, and I turn to see her pushchair hurtling down towards the water. I rush to catch it, and it stops in the reeds. Stephanie is strapped in, so at least I have done something right, but the incident scares me, and I am more careful in future. No one ever knows about the accident, I am too ashamed to tell.

These years of growing up, the times spent at Canal Road with my sister, Stephanie and Robert, are important years. They form the backbone of my future life, my ideas and opinions. I need to remember how Myrtle was, how Stephanie was, because it is only these memories that can sustain me in the future. Life does strange things to people. They change from being beautiful and happy, from singing and laughing, to becoming bitter and full of resentment. The lovely girl becomes the old lady without teeth who obsesses about dirty shoes on her carpet; the twisted adult who mourns her daughter, dead from cancer at forty. But, for now, the memory is bright, untarnished and beautiful.

Siblings are probably the most important people in our lives. Our ideas and beliefs are moulded by them. They are the beliefs we carry into adulthood. My brother remains, still, my rock and my example. His love of life, his indestructible optimism and energy are my inspiration. Writing now, we are all there is left, my brother and I. Mother, Father, sister — all dead now, with just memories and regrets to call upon. Clive still fills a room with his presence, he is still vital, full of life, energy and optimism, and I cannot imagine a life that doesn't have him in it. He is my mother, father, brother all in one person, and as I watch him, I can see them all. My last link with childhood and who I really am. The only person in the world who really, truly knows me.

Chapter Twenty-two

I am falling headlong down the slippery slope of adolescence. I escalate between extreme joy and intense despair. My clothes never feel right and I have a habit of flushing without warning. I spend my spare time walking around the town with my friend Hazel (or Willie, as I still call her), or riding bikes with Gill Rowstron . Gill rides on the outside because she has back lights, and because I wobble. We peddle along the Stoney Stanton road and I wobble into her, knocking her off. We tumble down together, and somehow I am picked up and driven home, while Gill, who has cut her knees, has to walk home alone. We cycle to the Co-op hall in Henley road for a dance, and I sit tongue-tied in a corner while Gill dances. I feel ungainly and self-conscious in my dress, distorted and huge inside my body.

Willie and I go together to a pub in Kenilworth, and I know that if my mother knew I would be in trouble. Pubs are forbidden because she is a Christadelphian. The pub is called the Engine, and boys with motor-bikes go there. This is why Willie likes to go. She is keen on one of the boys. We sit on the pillions of their bikes, and we roar down the Kenilworth road. This is so exciting! No helmets, they are not yet compulsory, so I feel my long hair streaming out behind me and I am in heaven.

There is a mixture of confidence and fear throughout

these times. One part of me has stepped into a young adult while the other part lingers reluctantly in childhood. Boys are a mystery, I fear them and yet I am fascinated. I watch Willie crying because a boy has finished with her, and wonder why she is upset. Why am I not experiencing these emotions?

Gill is meeting her boyfriend at the Saxon Mill, so we cycle there together. I linger by the waterfall, lean on a wall with my bike while Gill kisses her boyfriend. I should feel envious, but I am mesmerised by the endlessly falling water.

My job in the Purchasing Department of Courtaulds has begun, so I walk each day to the small office on Foleshill road. I have to learn shorthand and typing, but because there are no vacancies at the Technical College, I have to go there anyway and take Social Studies and History. This doesn't please me at all, but I go, and miraculously come out with marks in the 90s. Shorthand is to be learnt in special classes that I am to go to with Willie, my friend from school who is also working at Courtaulds. But we don't go! Instead, we catch a bus to Birmingham and have knickerbocker glories at Lewis's. The sheer delight of these stolen trips on the packed smoky bus on grey wet winter mornings comes abruptly to an end when we are found out, but it was worth it. We never do learn shorthand, but I survive well enough without it.

Willie is my special friend. We go to the Matrix every Saturday together, and go back home on the late bus. The boys sit at the back singing dirty songs, and I know all the words. We sleep at Willie's house because her mother doesn't mind. Willie is the only one, and the walls of their little council house are covered with photographs of her, red ringlets bouncing. Willie dances, tap dancing, and the photos are all of her dancing. I think she is very lucky. I want to dance, but never have the opportunity. We wake up in the morning to a shoe, disembodied, tapping on the bedroom window. We shriek loudly, and her mother, comes into the bedroom with the shoe that she had balanced on the line prop! There are many things like this that make us laugh. Willie's mother is waiting for us when we get in with a bowl of water for our aching feet. She listens to us talking about the boys, and she tells us, 'They all fart'. We laugh, but we don't believe her.

Willie smokes, but isn't supposed to, so she leans from her open bedroom window, blowing the smoke away, while I stand guard by the door in case her mother comes up the stairs. Though I have a go, it's a habit I never quite master. The smoke gets in my eyes and I choke.

I learn to type simply by using the typewriter in the office, so there are no more classes. Each week it is my job to walk along the Foleshill road to the print room, and I dread this trip. Don White works in the print room; he is an attractive boy who lives in Canal Road by Myrtle, and I become mute in his presence. He says rude things that make me redden and want to die. Things like, 'A girl went to see a doctor; he said "Big breathes" and she replied, "Yeth, and I'm only sixthteen"'. As I go to the door to make my escape, he calls me.

'Ehh!' he shouts. I turn, and he says, 'Ty one, eighty two'.

Now I am embarrassed and flustered again, so I run out clutching the papers.

When I go to visit my sister he is outside pouring petrol on the wall and burning it to kill the ants. I decide that I don't like boys at all.

I hate the office job; the enforced claustrophobic atmosphere of the tiny room, and the monotony of the job itself. My daydreams take me to nicer places where there isn't a CF Freeman to obey. CF is a kindly boss, though rather aloof. He leaves the running of the office to Daisy Hulbert, who adores him and protects him from us all. Daisy Hulbert is a tiny ferocious woman with a back deformity. She has never married, and CF is her whole life. I am a constant trial to her because I won't take orders and do as I am told to do. Joan Maughan is the senior girl in the office. She has just got married to Joe, and she keeps me and Pearl occupied by telling us in shy whispers about the intricacies of married life. We ask lots of questions, soaking it all up with indecent relish, but secretly I am not too sure about this stuff.

Another of my tasks is to go down to the canteen every day with a large tray and bring back tea for the men in the Drawing office. The canteen is warm and busy; it has a feel of home about it. The smell of cooking fills it, as stews and pies are made ready for lunchtime. Emma, a small round lady with grey hair in an untidy bun, fries onions in a huge pan, and the smell is delicious. Sausages fry in another huge pan, and I wait while she makes up the batches. I stagger back to the office with a loaded tray. A large metal teapot, milk and 16 mugs, and the batches. As I climb the stone steps to the drawing office, having already had to cope with the cat calls from the factory floor, I am approached by Jim Fenner. Women's rights are at this time unheard of, as he playfully tries to touch my bottom. He sees me as fair game, just a young girl. I am sixteen, unschooled in the ways of the world, but I am definitely not having this!

'If you touch me, I shall drop the tray,' I tell him.

FROM PARADISE TO EDEN

Laughter runs round the office, this is good sport, a young girl with fire in her eyes.

'No you won't,' he says, 'What would C.F. say'?

'Try me!' This time defiantly.

Jim Fenner touches my bottom, and I let go the tray at exactly the same moment.

Tray, teapot and mugs clatter down the stone steps, and I stand alone and unrepentant. Miss Daisy Hulbert marches me into her office. She is red-faced and flustered and completely at a loss to know what to do with a defiant, unrepentant sixteen-year-old. I am made to apologise to Mr Freeman, but I manage to make my point, that I will not be poked and prodded by these men. They treat me with much more respect after this incident.

Chapter Twenty-three

Away from work, dancing is what I now live for. As well as the studio with Alf and Hettie where I learn to ball-room dance for medals, I also go to the Matrix and Selbourne hall with Beryl and Jean Parker. Brothers Phil and Bob Startup go there too. My gawky feelings have disappeared; I am slim and graceful, noticed by Phil who wants a dancing partner. Inside the dance hall I am happy, but when a boy called George takes a fancy to me I am out of my depth. He is a nice, dark-eyed boy with black wavy hair, and he follows me everywhere. I panic – this is not what I want at all. Then there is Johnnie Hastie. He walks me home and I feel very comfortable, that is until I see my mother and Sister peeping from behind the curtain of the front room. They are laughing, and that is the end of Johnnie Hastie. I am ridiculous once more.

I have a circular skirt covered in tan flowers, that I wear with a tight black elastic waspy belt and three inch heels. Bill Haley is all the rage, and rock and roll is here. I jive all night, my skirt billowing out around me as I give myself over to the intoxicating rhythms. But it isn't always like this; there are dances at Courtaulds when I stand at the edge, isolated by my own difference until I retreat to the toilets. Locking myself in, I cry until my eyes are red and sore. Then I go home, to slip silently up the stairs before I am seen. Getting ready for one of these evenings,

I use powder for the first time. I feel so grown up as I walk into the sitting room. My dad, dear old Dad with his raw country upbringing, looks at me and says, 'You looks as if you've been sucking an old sow's tit'.

I run back to the security of my bedroom, leaving my Dad wondering what on earth is wrong with me. How could he ever understand that my confidence, already rock bottom, is now gone for ever.

The New Year's Eve dance is always the one with the most expectations, and the most let downs. That moment when they play the last waltz, the multi-mirrored orb in the centre of the ceiling turning slowly to throw rainbows of light across the dancer's faces, and I find myself dancing with a small spotty boy who treads all over my lovely silver three inch heel shoes. They release the balloons on the stroke of midnight, everyone rushing into the centre of the floor to gather as many as they can. This is where I slip away, my expectations unrealised. Full of disappointment and disillusionment, I limp slowly home. Late as usual, but no-one is worried. My parents are sound asleep as always. The streets are safe to walk in, I am untroubled as I walk along the deserted pavements.

My teenage years really are a kaleidoscope of emotion, of feeling different and on the outside. Not yet knowing what or who I am and always feeling that there is something more, something there just out of my sight, and I *will* find it soon. I sit in the front room for hours, pouring out my emotions onto my piano. Chopin preludes, the Warsaw concerto, Last Rhapsody, Dream of Olwyn. No one listens, and I am not surprised or upset. This is how life is – no expectancy, so no disappointment either.

By now I have been moved to the big office in the main building of Courtaulds. I sit in a typing pool with about twenty other girls, and there we are, all day, mindlessly typing out purchasing orders. We have to sit with a senior to check our work, and I dislike Dorothy intensely. She brings out the very worst in my belligerent nature, so I dread these daily sessions. I decide to try another tactic; I am pleasant to her, and she begins to warm towards me. I have learned another valuable lesson, and the checking sessions are more bearable.

Our typewriters are the old manual sort, so when the office is given just one new, electric typewriter, Mr Smallwood gives it to me. I am never sure why I am sin-gled out for this honour, but I value it none-the-less.

Mrs Prior, our over-seer, is a tall, elegant lady, gentle, with a very sad face. She wears the airforce wings on her tailored dresses and we are told that her husband was killed in the Dam-Buster's raid. I watch her wistful expression and long to say something to help, but I am just a typist, too young to know anything.

At lunch-time, we walk up and down the Foleshill Road to the cat calls of the men from the factory. I have a red woollen hat, and a red haired man shouts after me ' red hat – no drawers'. I am disgusted, yet attracted to this man with his half shut eyes and insolent manner. Willie knows him and introduces me to Bert Haywood. We be-come inseparable, and though my mother calls him a rough diamond, she warms toward him. Dad isn't so sure; this is his little girl and he doesn't trust anyone with her. Bert wears a scruffy tweed overcoat, his lovely red hair is in untidy curls in his neck. He always has a cigarette in the corner of his mouth, and I think he is wonderful. He makes me feel safe and cared for. We go a lot to the Continental café in Corporation street where we sit with frothy coffee in pyrex cups. He also takes me to 'The Nugget', a pub in

Coundon. I am very uncomfortable here, even though I have been taken to the pub on Foleshill road called 'The General Wolfe' by my sister and her husband. I sit, straight backed and disapproving while a man called Ossie sings a rude song about Old King Cole. I have one half of shandy and sip it slowly, looking as out of place as I feel. We meet Mick and Monica, friends of Bert, and they think I am 'posh' because I sit so straight and look disapproving. Still, they become friends, and it is Monica, who as a midwife, helps my first grandchild Emma Louise into the world.

I spend all my spare time with Bert, giving up the cheap piano lessons from Mr Hurst and letting go the first of my many chances. My lessons with Mr Hurst had come about because of the visit to Earlsdon where I played the white grand piano. I was to have the lessons half-price for a year in order to reach the standard needed for the youth Orchestra, and I let it all go. Maybe when you are brought up to expect nothing because you are 'working-class', you stop aspiring higher. I feel that I don't deserve it, that they must be wrong about my abilities.

Within a year, Bert and I are married. The year is tinged with sadness, as my father is in Lee House recovering from a total breakdown. His bleak childhood, the horror of the trenches in the First World War at sixteen, the loss of his arm, have all culminated in his mental shut-down. I go with my mother to visit him, walking through Kenilworth to catch the bus. He comes out to see us, his face is crumpled, his eyes sunk into their sockets as if he doesn't want to see. His jacket is hanging loose, and I have no words for him. I try though, talking about my wedding. He remains silent until we move to go, then, I watch as tears slide slowly down his grey-yellow furrowed cheeks, and my heart hurts.

The months before our wedding are spent saving money and planning. Bert walks from Coundon to see me every Sunday afternoon, and brings me 'Merry maid' toffees. We go for walks into town, not using the bus because we need the money.

My father is home, just in time for my wedding. He will give me away. We spend the night before our wedding with Mick and Monica, decorating the living room of our rented house. We all sing 'Bread of Heaven' as we paint, and it is very late before we finish.

In the morning, I put on my satin crinoline style dress, my little hat and veil, and leave the house for St.Paul's church with my dad. He looks haggard and drawn as he leads me up the aisle, and I love him all the more because of his suffering.

Outside the church we walk happily beneath an archway made by firemen. Our wedding is joyful and hopeful. Six weeks after our wedding, Bert goes into the army to do his National Service.

Chapter Twenty-four

Our home is the rented house next door to my mother. It has no electricity, so I use candles until Myrtle's husband Len fixes me one light bulb on the end of a long flex. Our floors are bare quarry tiles, and my kitchen furniture is made from orange boxes that I have made pretty with gingham curtains. We buy a second hand brown Rexine couch, and I have the old chair from my mother.

During the first few months of being there without Bert, I continue to walk along Broad Street to work each day, becoming more and more withdrawn. I am now convinced that everyone is talking about me, and I retreat even more into myself. At home I am not eating properly. I have never looked after myself before; I am eighteen and like a child. My mother believes I have made my bed, so I must lie on it. Alarm bells ring at work, and the nurse arranges for me to go to a convalescent home in North Wales. This is my first break-down, though I don't recognise it as such at the time. I wait every day for a letter from Bert, which always comes, and I write to him every day. Nothing has ever been this painful. Nothing has prepared me for this.

Always forbidden to have animals at home, I now take on an unruly dog and a stray kitten. Mickey wrecks what little home we have, and Boo Boo is no better. But I can have them can't I! This is *my* home now. My mother comes round to tell me that I MUST get rid of them, and I think 'she can't say that any more'.

But Mickey goes to another home, where they can look after him properly. I have a lot to learn about life and about animals.

We have been married for one year and three months when I find that I am pregnant. I am delighted, but my mother isn't. Bert gets home every weekend, hitch-hiking because we can't afford train fare. The weeks are hard; I am still working, walking both ways, and we still have orange boxes, a bucket for the washing, and our outside toilet with no bathroom. Not that it is missed. How can it be when I have never had one. I now eat my sketchy meals from the saucepan, I can't be bothered to dish it out properly. When the darkness comes, I sit on the bare, dark wooden stairs holding my bulb, too afraid to go up or go down. My health is suffering so Doctor Wilson tells my mother to take me back home for a while until Bert is demobbed. She does this reluctantly, and also cooks my meal, but charges me one shilling and threepence for it. I believe this is her way of making me grow up, but it isn't helpful. It isn't the last time I meet with her unbending will and lack of compassion. Her phrase of 'You made your bed, now lie on it' is said many more times.

Our beautiful daughter Laurie is born in May 1958. Bert is still hitch-hiking home from Kineton every night, and leaving at six in the morning. He is at home when I go into labour. We have no phone or car, so he cycles to the phone box to call for Nurse Brett from Awson Street. She doesn't believe him when he says that my pains are every five minutes, so he cycles to Awson street to convince her. Bert waits downstairs boiling water while my dear friend Kathie's mother Mrs Evans, Gladys, stays with me. She is with me and the midwife until Laurie is born at six in the morning. I am happy; Bert is happy; I now feel that I have everything in the world. My sister comes to look after me every day, making me my favourite egg custard in pastry, and Bert is demobbed. What more could I possibly want, my life is complete. I have no carpets or furniture, no fridge or microwave oven, no washing machine or car, no hot water or bathroom, and yet my cup flows over with happiness.

Every day I soak my terry towelling nappies in one bucket, then put them to boil in another bucket on the old gas stove. I hang them on the line in my tiny yard, put my exquisite little daughter in her second hand pram, and I feel totally happy and at peace.

Bert is home now and working in the fire service. He earns £9.00 a week, so I put away our rent money, electric and gas just the way my mother does. Our treat at the weekend is to walk into town with Laurie in the pram, and share a cup of coffee in the café. We now have an allotment on the Foleshill road. We leave my mother looking after Laurie, and set off on the bus with our spade and fork. These summer evenings are full of contentment as we dig and plant, weed and water.

It is now that we have our very first television set. My parents get one just before I leave home, but watching the tiny screen in darkness is a limited pleasure. Now we have our very own, and even the intermission picture is an excitement.

On Friday mornings I shop, then I come back to scrub my front step because this is what women do in 1958. It is what my mother does. Our baby girl is perfect, we have a black cat called Boo Boo, and life has a comfortable pattern.

I don't know it yet, but this is only the very beginning of a journey that is to become a living nightmare, where I awake from one dream only to fall into another. A deep dark abyss from which there seems no escape or ending.

The next story will be long in its telling.

I have journeyed backwards in time to the streets of my childhood. Experienced for the second time, a simple life, where despite hardship and trauma, each day had its predictable pattern. I have looked through the eyes of a small girl and seen the warmth of the people who wove the fabric of my growing years. It has been a long trip, moving through dark tunnels of memories to a city ravaged by war, and back again to the point at which I began

Here in Shap village, nestling comfortably in the valley of Eden, white hills seem to float above grey mist. Sun, deep amber fading into palest peach is mirrored on ice-white fields. Streams rushing down jagged rocks have frozen. Stopped in their joyful rush downwards, suspended, they are transformed into vast shining icicles, caught in the spell of winter.

As I sit and look back over my life, its beginnings and its struggles, just for a moment, fleeting, in my mind I see a gate; a faded rose the colour of crushed pink velvet tumbling over blue bars. A path winding up towards a door; columbine and honeysuckle tumbling across its uneven stones. My reluctant thoughts move into the present time, releasing childhood to embrace again the years in between.

Here, village life moves at a steady and gentle pace. It flows between the Post Office and the local Co-operative shop; the Doctor's surgery and the coffee shop. There are friendly greetings, smiles on familiar faces, and a daily rhythm of life that fits comfortably around me. Children's voices carry as they chase in the playground just the way I did all those years ago in a different place. On snowy fields they slide and throw snowballs. In summer months they climb, run and play in streams. They are safe here, and life is good for them.

I have returned home; this village, so similar in its essence to the Paradise of my childhood, has allowed me to belong. I grew up in a community of people who cared more for each other than for material wealth. Respect and politeness were important. Mister Barker always raised his hat to my mother when they passed each other in the street. People valued each other, they valued life because life had been threatened. We knew as small children, that adults were in control; we had guidelines, and they felt safe. We could move within them, knowing always just how far we could go. I have found the same values in Shap. My journey has truly been from Paradise… to Eden.